How to Add Ten Years to your Life and to Double Its Satisfactions

S. S. Curry

Writat

This edition published in 2021

ISBN : 9789390439508

Design and Setting By
Writat
(An Imprint of Vij Publishiing Group)
www.vijbooks.in
contact@vijpublishing.com

Contents

Can you wake as wake the birds?
In their joy and singing share?
Stretch your limbs as do the herds,
And drink as deep the morning
air?
Quick as larks on upward wing,
Can you shun the demon's wiles,
Promptly as the robins sing,
Can you change all frowns to
smiles?
Can you spurn fear's coward whine,
Meet each day with joyous song?
Then will angels guard your shrine,
Joys be deep and life be long.

To Those Who
Loyally Responded to The Dream
And to Those Who
By Thought, Word or Act Will Aid
The School of Expression
To Perform Its Important Function In Education.

QUI TRANSTULIT SUSTINET

As ancient exile at the close of day,
Paused on his country's farthest hills to view
Those valleys sinking in the distant blue
Where all the joys and hopes of childhood lay
;So now across the years our thoughts will stray
To those whose hearts were ever brave and true,
Who gave the hope and faith from which we
Drew
The strength to climb thus far upon our way.
As he amid the rocks and twilight gray,
Saw rocks and steeps transform to stairs, and
Knew
He wandered not alone; so may we too
See this, our tentless crag where wild winds play
A Bethel rise, and we here wake to know
That down and upward angels come and go.

WHY AND WHEREFORE

When over eighty years of age, the poet Bryant said that he had added more than ten years to his life by taking a simple exercise while dressing in the morning. Those who knew Bryant and the facts of his life never doubted the truth of this statement.

I have made inquiries lately among men who are eighty years of age, as to their method of waking up. Almost without exception, I find that they have been in the habit of taking simple exercise upon rising and also before retiring.

While studying voice in Paris, over thirty years ago, my teacher was so busy that he had to take me before breakfast at an hour which, to a Parisian, was a very early one.

"Vocal exercises may be more difficult at this time," he said, "but it is the best time. If we can start the day with the right exercise of the voice, the use of it all through the day will be additional right practice."

Later, when I studied with the elder Lamperti in Italy, I requested and secured an early hour in the morning for my lessons.

In teaching I have always urged students to take their exercises the first thing in the morning. Those who have taken my advice have later been grateful for the suggestion.

If my own morning exercises are neglected, I feel as if I had missed a meal or had lost much sleep. I was never what is called physically strong; in fact, physicians have continually prophesied my downfall, yet all my life I have performed about three men's work, and by the use of a few exercises have probably doubled the length of my life.

The subject of human development has always been of great interest to me. I have tried to investigate the various systems of gymnastics in all countries; and, teaching, as I have, about ten thousand the use of the voice and body in expression, I have studied training from a different point of view from that of most men.

I have discovered that the voice cannot be adequately trained without also improving the body; that the improvement of the voice can be doubly accelerated if the body is considered a factor.

I have also found, what is more important, that true exercises are all mental and emotional and not physical, and that both body and voice can never be truly improved except by right thinking and feeling.

I, therefore, long ago came to certain conclusions which are not in accordance with common views. My convictions, however, have been the result, not only of experience, but of wide study and investigation.

This book embodies a few points about health; without going deeply into the principles involved, a short programme is given, the practice of which has already accomplished marvelous results. The book embodies my own experiences, and obeys the scientific principles involved in training.

It is meant to be a guide for home study and practice. The principles are applicable to everyone. It requires at first, patience, perseverance, and resolution at that moment in the day when we are most liable to be indifferent and negative, if not irresolute and discouraged. Whoever resolutely undertakes to obey the suggestions will never regret doing so. In fact, it is not too much to claim that he will not only lengthen his life but double its satisfactions.

Every reader of the book is requested to become a member of the Morning League, and whosoever does so and makes a report or writes to me fully about special weaknesses, habits, "besetting sins," or conditions will receive a letter of suggestions.

This book and its companion, "The Smile," are published as a part of the great work undertaken by the friends of the School of Expression; the net receipts from the sale will go to the Endowment Fund of the institution.

I.
SIGNIFICANCE OF MORNING

"The year's at the spring
And day's at the morn;
Morning's at seven;
The hill-side's dew-pearled;
The lark's on the wing;
The snail's on the thorn;
God's in his heaven—
All's right with the world!"

Song from "Pippa Passes"
Robert Browning

Browning's "Pippa Passes" is a parable or allegory of human life.

Though called a drama by its author, it embodies, like all plays of the highest type, other than dramatic elements. In exalted poetry the allegoric, lyric, epic and dramatic seem to be blended. An effort to separate them often seems academic and mechanical.

Pippa, a poor little silk-winding girl, who has never known father or mother, opens the poem. It is the early morning and she wakes with joyous anticipation of her holiday, her only one. She goes forth, and we hear her singing and we see her influencing, from her humble position in the background, "Asolo's four happiest ones," who are brought by the action of the drama into the foreground.

Her character and that of the other persons of the play are well-defined; but the real theme of the poem is the unconscious influence that she exerts upon others. The primary element of dramatic art is the meeting of people and the influence they exert upon each other. There is no direct influence seemingly exerted upon Pippa herself save at one point and even that is scarcely a conscious one.

We feel that she is a type of the human soul. Specific scenes, though intensely dramatic, are entirely separated from one another.

Accordingly if it is a drama, it is a drama of an unusual type. It regards the events of only one day; still that day is not literal; it is a symbol of the life of everyone. It is New Year's Day, but every day is the beginning of a new year. It is a holiday, yet all life, when normally lived, is dominated by love and sympathetic service, and is full of happiness.

Pippa sings as everyone should sing with the spirit of thanksgiving and love. She welcomes the day with joy as everyone should welcome life and its opportunities. She lies down to sleep at night, as we all do; her sun drops into a "black cloud" and she knows nothing of what she has really accomplished or of the revelation that is coming on the morrow.

Moreover, observe that the link of unity in the play is found in the songs of Pippa. One might easily conceive her beautiful character as embodying the very soul of lyric poetry. Hence, in reading the poem, we are impressed from the first with allegoric, lyric and epic, as well as dramatic elements.

Observe more closely her awakening. Note the beautiful description, the gradually lengthening lines, indicative of the coming morning.

She expresses joy as she meditates over her New Year's hymn. Into this devotional lyric Browning has breathed the spirit of all true life and service.

"Now wait!—even I already seem to share
In God's love: what does New-year's hymn declare?
What other meaning do these verses bear?

All service ranks the same with God:
If now, as formerly he trod
Paradise, his presence fills
Our earth, each only as God wills
Can work—God's puppets, best and worst,
Are we; there is no last nor first.

Say not "a small event!" Why "small"?
Costs it more pain that this, ye call
A "great event," should come to pass,
Than that? Untwine me from the mass
Of deeds which make up life, one deed
Power shall fall short in, or exceed!

And more of it, and more of it! oh, yes—
I will pass each, and see their happiness,
And envy none—being just as great, no doubt,
Useful to men, and dear to God, as they!
A pretty thing to care about
So mightily, this single holiday!

But let the sun shine! Wherefore repine?
—With thee to lead me, O Day of mine,
Down the grass path grey with dew,
Under the pine-wood, blind with boughs,
Where the swallow never flew
Nor yet cicala dared carouse—
No, dared carouse!"

From "Pippa Passes"
Robert Browning

As Pippa leaves her room in the full spirit of this hymn, full of joy, hope and love, she passes into the street. We hardly catch a glimpse of her until the close of the day, when she comes back and lies down to sleep: but we hear her songs and see the influence which she unconsciously exerts. This is the real theme of the poem.

Browning's poetic play reveals to us in four scenes the other side of life, the happier people to whom Pippa referred in her soliloquy. We look first into the interior of the old house of which Pippa has spoken with a kind of awe, and see the proud Ottima who owns the mills where Pippa is but a poor worker. In the dark gloom of one of the rooms Ottima has become the sharer in a murder, and, under the influence of Pippa's song, which is heard outside, she and her companion realize their guilt and are overcome with remorse.

At noon we are introduced to a young artist, Jules, who is just bringing home his bride, Phene, whom he has married thinking her a princess, but who is really a poor, ignorant child. She has been employed unconsciously, to herself, and innocently used by some degraded artists as a means of rebuking the idealist, Jules. By this cruel trick they mean to crush him and reduce him to their own sensual level. Even letters which Jules has received from the supposed princess have been written by these perversions of human beings—who call themselves artists.

In her lovely innocence Phene is thrilled by Jules' tenderness. Her intuition tells her that something is wrong as she falters in rendering the lines the cruel painters have given her to read to Jules.

We see the blow fall upon the young dreamer as he makes the fearful discovery. In the agony of his disappointment he is about to renounce Phene forever as the artists, waiting outside to sneer at him, expect. The poor, innocent being, in whom his kindness and tenderness have stirred to life for the first time her womanly nature, is about to be cast out to a life of degradation and misery, when Pippa passes, singing. Her song awakens Jules to a higher feeling, to a more human and heroic determination; and the painters, waiting outside, are disappointed.

In the evening Pippa passes Luigi, an Italian patriot. He is meditating over the afflictions of his country and upon a plan to help it, while his mother is trying to dissuade him from the daring undertaking. The police and spies are waiting outside. If he goes he will not be arrested; if he stays they have orders to arrest him at once. At the moment of his wavering, when he is almost ready to obey his mother, Pippa's song arouses anew his patriotic being, and he resolutely goes forth to do a true heroic deed for his country. Thus Pippa saves him from imprisonment and death.

Night brings the last scene in the dramatic events of the world influenced by Pippa's songs. A room of the "palace by the Dome," of which Pippa seems to stand in so much awe, opens before us. Here we look into the face of the Monsignor, for whom she expressed reverence in the morning, and we find that the Monsignor and the dead brother whose home he comes to bless, are in reality Pippa's own uncles. The poor little girl, with only a nickname, is a child of an older brother and the real heir to the Palace, though of this she has never had the remotest dream. We see an insinuating villain tempting the Monsignor to allow him to do away with Pippa in a most horrible manner, and thus leave the Monsignor in sole possession of his brother's property.

During an intense moment Pippa passes and her singing outside causes her uncle to throttle the villain and call for help.

Then we see, at the close of the day, the little girl, unconscious of her share in the life of others, come back to her room and fall asleep murmuring her New Year's hymn which, in spite of appearances, she still trusts. We are left with the hope that she will awaken next day to realize who she is and come into her own.

Thus journey we all through life often forgetting that there is nothing small, that "there is no last nor first." We are conscious of noble aims, but oblivious of the real work we are doing and of our own identity.

What, do you ask, has such a poetic drama to do with such a commonplace subject as health or the prolonging of life?

The question implies a misconception. Human development is not a material thing but is poetic and exalted. It has to do not merely with physical conditions but primarily with spiritual ideals. Let us observe more closely how Browning wakes Pippa up. When she comes to consciousness she utters a cry of joy and thanksgiving;

> "Day!
> Faster and more fast,
> O'er night's brim, day boils at last."

The joyous thanksgiving of this first moment is the key to Pippa's life and to her influence through the whole day. Such was the right beginning to her day and such is the right beginning for us all to every day of our lives. Her faith and her hymn revealed the true ideals of this strange journey we call life.

There is an old proverb: "Guard beginnings." If a stream is poisoned at its head it will carry the deadly taint through its whole course.

The most significant moment of life is the moment of awakening.

The importance of morning has been more or less realized in the instinct of the human heart in every age.

Many of the myths of the early Greeks refer to the miracle of the morning. Aurora mirrors to us in a mystic way the significance of this hour to the Greeks. Athene was born by the stroke of the hammer of Hephæstus on the forehead of Zeus, and thus the stroke of fire upon the sky became the symbol or myth of all civilization. Even Daphne, pursued by Apollo, and turned into a tree, is doubtless the darkness fleeing before dawn until the trees stand out clearly defined in the morning light.

The dawn of day has always been considered a prophecy of the time when all ignorance will vanish before the light of truth.

When we remember that men of the early ages had no other light but that of the sun, we can see how naturally the coming of morning impressed primitive peoples, and it is not much wonder that they adored and worshiped the dawn and the rising sun.

We still speak of the dawn of a new civilization. Morning is still the most universal figure of progress, the type of a new life. More than all other natural occurrences it is used as a symbol of something higher.

May we not, accordingly, discover that from a psychological as well as a physiological point of view, for reasons of health and development, morning is the most significant and important time of the day!

No human being at the first moment of awakening is gloomy or angry. Everyone awakes in peace with all the world. It is a time of freedom. A moment later memory may bring to the mind some scene or picture that leads to good or bad thought, followed by emotion. This first moment of consciousness is the critical and golden moment of human life. How often has it been said to a child: "You must have gotten out of the wrong side of bed this morning."

Even animals and birds feel the significance of morning. Who has not, at early dawn, heard a robin or some other bird begin to sing—"at first alone," as Thomas Hardy says, "as if sure that morning has come, while all the others keep still a moment as if equally sure that he is mistaken." Soon, however, voice after voice takes up the song until the whole woodland is ringing with joyous tones. Who, in such an hour, has not been deeply moved with the spirit and beauty of all life and the harmony and deep significance of all of nature's processes?

If we observe the awaking of birds and animals more carefully, however, we find something besides songs.

All the higher animals go through certain exercises on first waking. There seems a universal instinct which teaches that certain stretches, expansions and deep breathings are necessary at this time. In fact, these actions are so deeply implanted in the instinct of animals that they seem a kind of sacred acceptance of life, a species of thanksgiving for all that life brings.

If we accept "Pippa Passes" as a parable of human life and Pippa as a typical human being, may we not in her awakening find an example of this universal instinct? May we not find her first thoughts and feelings worthy of study and her example one to be followed? Do we not, in fact, find here a beautiful illustration of the proper mode of meeting the sacredness of dawn?

As a matter of fact, how do we actually greet the morning? Do we awake as Pippa did, with a joyous song of praise? Do we pour out our hearts in gratitude that it brings a new day, a new life? Do we give thanks for the new opportunities given us, the new possibilities of enjoyment, the new share in the life of the world?

Usually we have no thought about these things. Most of us entirely forget the significance of the way or "the side we get out of bed."

Attention is rarely paid to the spirit in which we awaken children. It is often by means of an angry demand or an indulgent whine. They rise with the impression that it is a sin to awaken them and they begin the day with the feeling that the world is cruel.

If we could spend the first few moments of every morning as Pippa spent her first moments, the character of the whole life would be determined. It is the most important time of every day. Is it not also the time when we are most apt to be tempted?

Has not man seemingly lost the significance of this sacred hour? Why do so many, on waking up, begin to worry over the difficulties of the day? How many look back with regret to the preceding day and forward with a frown to the one newly born! Why not smile as Pippa smiled and meet our blessings with thanksgiving?

There are certain physiological reasons why people feel so sluggish on first awaking:—the position in bed is cramped, the limbs are contracted, the circulation is impeded and the breathing is greatly hindered. When lying down, all the functions of the vital organs are lessened.

Many people are entirely too careless regarding the air of the room. It needs to be even purer and fresher during one's hours of repose than in those of waking.

Certain simple movements are taken by practically every animal on awaking under normal conditions. Among these are yawning, deep breathing, expansion and stretching. These exercises form a part of the process of awaking. It is the change from the position of lying down to that of standing up. But we find that man rarely takes these exercises. Between the moment of awakening and standing erect man possibly takes more time, whines more and does less than any other animal.

Of all the provisions of nature to meet this crucial moment in animal life the stretch seems to be most important. Why men neglect the stretch is curious. Man seems to lack something of the vigor of the animal instinct on awakening. He lives a more rational life, and it is necessary for him at this time to make certain decisions and exert firmness and resolution.

Science has carefully explained the stretch, but men seem to refuse to take the lesson. The stretch extends the body so that the veins, where congestion is most liable to take place and where pressure of blood is weakest, are so elongated that the blood flows more easily from the arteries, where the pressure is strongest, through the veins back to the heart and circulation is equalized and stimulated.

The beneficial effects of the stretch can be felt by anyone who will take the pains on waking up in the morning to stretch easily, for a few minutes, then rest a few moments and note the effect. He will feel a great exhilaration all through the body. He will feel a sense of harmony. Thanksgiving seems to arise from every cell at the fresh blood and life.

The yawn is similar to the stretch. The yawn is a stretch of the lungs as the stretch is a yawn of the muscles. Both of these exercises express a hunger for oxygen. Whenever anyone is sitting in a cramped position or even in one position for a long time, the stretch or yawn is instinctive. The extension of the muscles of the body as illustrated in the stretch is one of the most necessary steps in normal adjustment. To speak of only one point: when a man sits his knees are bent, and the muscles in front of the leg are elongated and the muscles back of the knee are shortened. A stretch means simply the extension of these shortened muscles.

All over the body we find a tendency to elongate certain muscles too much. This is true in the chest; true also of the face, at the corners of the mouth. The active use of the too elongated muscles will produce extension in those that are too much shortened. By doing this we bring about certain normal conditions and relations of parts.

Again we find that the stretch is activity of the extensor muscles. It is the action of the extensor muscles upon which health especially depends. At any rate, the extensor muscles are much more important to bring about the right relation of all parts and the right balance of sensitive muscles and the equalization of circulation than the activity of the flexor muscles. Normal emotions, as we shall find later, are expressed through activity of the extensor muscles. Abnormal emotions, such as anger, affect the flexor muscles of the body more.

Since nature has provided the stretch seemingly as the antidote for abnormal position, and especially abnormal position during sleep, in the programme of exercises it would seem most necessary to centre around some careful and scientific use of stretches.

Have you ever noticed a dog or cat wake up? Observe their instinctive movements: the gradual but vigorous stretch in every direction, the deep breathing, the sympathetic extension and staying of the limbs at the climax, then the gradual giving up of the activity and the moment of restful satisfaction.

Stretching in this way is one of the primitive instincts in all animals. He who will observe the animals will feel that the time for practicing the exercises is on awakening, and the primary exercise to be taken is the stretch.

How can we best occupy a part at least of the half hour or more that is usually wasted in worrying and fretting or in sluggish indifference, between the time when we first awake and the time we begin to dress? With all the knowledge of the human organism which has been revealed to us by modern science, with our truer understanding of the nature of men, of the effect of the mind upon the body, with our observation of the instinctive actions of the animals at such an hour, why can we not so occupy a few of these most precious moments of the day as to add to our vitality and enjoyment?

At this moment of awakening, when your mind is free, you can so direct your attention as to receive joy instead of gloom, love instead of hate. You can exclude the thought of evil or you can yield and allow the tempter to desecrate your shrine. Whichever choice you make, these first moments of your day's living will color the whole course of the coming hours. The feeling first accepted and welcomed will more or less continue and form a background to all your ideas and determine your point of view toward human events.

The chief aim of this book is to present a simple programme giving, not only some exercises for this hour, but certain explanations which will inspire a sense of the importance of this hour and these movements.

Most people have no conception of the possibilities of human nature, of the fact that progress is the highest characteristic of a human being. No matter how old we are, we can always begin to climb upward; the main thing is our willingness to climb. Do we understand how to use the least actions and the most neglected movements for the development of character and the satisfactions of life?

The principles and exercises advocated in this book are not extravagant. Again and again their benefits have been proven and many thereby have doubled life's satisfactions and its length.

II.
SUPPOSED SECRETS OF HEALTH AND LONG LIFE

Before laying down a simple programme which will give one a common sense method of keeping well, living long, and making the very most of life, it may be well to study some of the innumerable theories regarding long life.

If all the discussions upon health and long life, from the earliest time to the present, could be adequately chronicled they would form an interesting, if not an amusing history. In many of these, however, we should find the same serious thoughts which we may well consider and find by comparison a few points in which all agree as to what is necessary to health, happiness and length of days. Note the theories that have been seriously advocated and which have had vogue among certain classes for a time,—such as the use of cold water every day as a remedy for all diseases. The cold water cure advocated wet sheet packs for fevers, and water, in some form, for all ailments. To live long some physicians have advised sleeping on the right side, others have advocated the use of raw food or food that has been cooked very slightly. Some have contended that scientific food is the complete food found in Nature, such as nuts; still others have advocated whole wheat bread!

In our own time a method has been emphasized which has been called "Fletcherizing." This, of course, is taken from the name of the gentleman, who has made it so illustrious by his books and his discussions of the subject. Mr. Fletcher's principle consists in holding or masticating the food until it is in a fluid form; even a liquid must be held in the mouth until it is of the same temperature as that of the body.

Many consider that the chief advantage of Fletcherizing is that it makes a person eat less. This may be a part of the advantage.

I once had the honor of sitting at dinner by the side of Mr. Fletcher and observed his methods. He did not eat more than one-third of the amount, for example, of ice-cream that the rest ate, but he stopped when the others did, and said, with a smile:—"I have had enough; what I have eaten will give me more nourishment than a larger amount would and it will not give me any trouble."

There is great truth in some of these theories. We should eat less meat and more grain. We should not bolt the best food elements out of wheat; we should not bleach rice and take out its nutritious element. Certainly, our lives are very unscientific. Most men live merely by accident. The shortness of life is not surprising to one who understands how irrationally most of us live.

Others say, breathe deeply, naturally and constantly.

Still others have urged active life out of doors or an active participation in business. It is a well-known fact that many men have not lived long after retiring from their occupations.

Andrew Carnegie said recently that he attributed his long life, health and strength to his activity. The story is told that he walked the floor of his room with deep anxiety and consternation the night after his offer was accepted to sell the Carnegie Steel Works. He had not thought it possible that his price would be accepted, and he kept speaking to his old friend about the amount of money paid and the greatness of the responsibility. Fortunately he did not retire, as most men do, but took an interest in every phase of modern life. He has used his money, as a sacred trust, according to his own best judgment, building libraries and giving organs, pensioning teachers who have given their lives for truth rather than for making money, and has furthered many other causes.

One of the most common opinions is that long life depends upon "our constitution,"—upon what we receive from our ancestors. That is, long life is a gift, not an attainment. And we are in the habit of blaming our ancestors, near and remote, for our lack of strength and vitality.

Dr. Oliver Wendell Holmes once made the remark that if one wished to live a long life he should be afflicted with some incurable disease. This was thought to be merely a joke, but it has foundation in fact. Many men with poor constitutions live to a very advanced age. They study themselves and live simply. They realize that they are not strong and they do not indulge themselves, but reach out for health and strength in all ways.

Among all the practices which men have adopted through different ages for prolonging life we find many which are universally believed, though possibly not practiced. Some discussion of these may give us courage and enable us to realize how unscientifically, how carelessly, most men live, and how indifferent we really are to our well-being.

And yet we find wide-spread doubt as to the advisability of being too fastidious. Some of the extravagant ideas have naturally given rise to such scepticism.

On hardly any subject have men had such extreme views as they have regarding health or the prolongation of their own lives.

I know one lady who ate a raw carrot every morning because it was yellow, and, as yellow is a spiritual color, this practice, it was advocated, would free one from materiality and, consequently, from all disease.

I have known others who condemned all attention to proper food, exercise, and even to expression, because such attention would lead to faith in material means.

Webster said, "Truth is always congruous, and agrees with itself; every truth in the universe agrees with every other truth in the universe; whereas falsehoods not only disagree with truth but usually quarrel among themselves."

In accordance with this principle as a rule the untruthfulness of any view is seen in its failure to recognize anything else as true.

No one will advocate any extreme and irrational habit. Too much attention to food, too much attention to the care of the body and exercise will degrade even character. The morning exercises which are here recommended should be taken even as one washes his hands, as a matter of course. Man is spiritual, and character is developed spiritually, and mere attention to the body does not secure health and strength.

There is a great and easily demonstrated truth in the fact that people who believe in a spiritual life have endured untold hardships and have faced all kinds of conditions without injury. The power of mind over body, of spirit over matter, is too well attested to be doubted.

However, man is slow and progress must be made gradually. The first step must be taken before the last can be taken. Extravagant and wrong views prevent a great many people from doing anything.

If we examine all the rules for securing health and the leading secrets of long life, we find that one of the earliest is temperance.

A noted instance is Socrates. During the great plague, when at least one-third of the population of Athens died, Socrates went about with impunity. This was no doubt due to the cheerfulness and temperance of his life. We know of his cheerfulness from accounts by Zenophon and Plato.

Possibly the most illustrious example, which has been recounted of the preservation of health and the prolonging of life through temperance, is Luigi Cornaro, who was born in Venice in 1464. After having, according to Gamba, wasted his youth, his health was so broken and his habits so fixed that "upon passing the age of thirty-five he had nothing left to hope for but that he might end in death the suffering of a worn-out life."

This man, by resolution and temperance, battled with his perverted habits and became strong and vigorous and happy, and lived to be over one hundred years of age. "The good old man," said Graziani, "feeling that he drew near the end, did not look upon the great transit with fear, but as though he were about to pass from one house into another. He was seated in his little bed—he used a small and very narrow one—and, at its side, was his wife, Veronica, almost his equal in years. In a clear and sonorous voice he told me why he would be able to leave this life with a valiant soul.... Feeling a little later the failure of vital force, he exclaimed, 'Glad and full of hope will I go with you, my good God!' He then composed himself; and having closed his eyes, as though about to sleep, with a slight sigh, he left us forever."

A new edition of Cornaro's discourses on the temperate life, by William F. Butler of Milwaukee, has recently been issued under the title of "The Art of Living Long." The first of these discourses was written at the age of eighty-three, the second at eighty-six, the third at ninety-one, and the fourth at ninety-five. His treatises have been popular for all these centuries.

He held that the older a man grows the wiser he becomes and the more he knows; and if he will, by temperance and regularity of life and exercise, preserve his strength, his powers of enjoyment will grow, as his own did, every year until the end.

"Men are, as a rule," says Cornaro, "very sensual and intemperate, and wish to gratify their appetites and give themselves up to the commission of innumerable disorders. When, seeing that they cannot escape suffering the unavoidable consequences of such intemperance as often as they are guilty of it, they say—by way of excuse—that it is preferable to live ten years less and to enjoy life. They do not pause to consider what immense importance ten years more of life, and especially of healthy life, possess when we have reached mature age, the time, indeed, at which men appear to the best advantage in learning and virtue—two things which can never reach their perfection except with time. To mention nothing else at present, I shall only say that, in literature and in the sciences, the majority of the best and most celebrated works we possess were written when their authors had attained ripe age, and during these same ten latter years for which some men, in order that they may gratify their appetites, say they do not care."

We see not only in this passage but in many other places evidence of the fact that Cornaro lived a cheerful, contented life. The reform was evidently not merely in his eating and drinking but fully as much in the inner thought of his life. This is shown in many passages from his discourses.

He says: "Although reason should convince them that this is the case, yet these men refuse to admit it, and pursue their usual life of disorder as heretofore. Were they to act differently, abandoning their irregular habits and adopting orderly and temperate ones, they would live to old age—as I have—in good condition. Being, by the grace of God, of so robust and perfect a constitution, they would live until they reached the age of a hundred and twenty, as history points out to us that others—born, of course, with perfect constitutions—have done, who led the temperate life.

"I am certain I, too, should live to that age had it been my good fortune to receive a similar blessing at my birth; but, because I was born with a poor constitution, I fear I shall not live much beyond a hundred years."

According to the census of the United States not one man in twenty thousand attains the age of one hundred years. If we figure out carefully from these statistics, we find the average is only about one-third of this period of life.

One of the social customs is that we must eat an extraordinary meal,—far more than we need, as if life's enjoyment depended on the low sense of taste,—as if every contract or matter of important business must have this as an introduction. Theoretically speaking, many people believe in low living and high thinking, but it is very rare that we find one who practices it.

The two simple rules of Cornaro deserve our attention: to eat only what he wanted, that is, what he actually needed for the sustenance of his body, and to eat only those things which really agreed with him, that is, those which were really helpful to the sustenance of his life. If we should consider eating merely as a means and not an end, Cornaro's idea that the normal age of a human being was one hundred and twenty years would not be such a wild dream.

Another almost universally recognized requisite is exercise in the open air, or regular, systematic, simple and vigorous activity of some kind.

The necessity of thoroughly pure air must be emphasized from first to last. Some think that the dullness felt by many people in the early morning is due to the impure air of cities, and to the failure to open windows. A lady once said to me, "When I am in the country I always sleep out of doors. Then I have not the slightest disinclination to get up. I do it as naturally and as gladly as the animals."

It is to be hoped that the rapid transit and the automobile will enable people to live farther out in the country, farther from air poisoned by smoke and gases. Even in cities, however, one may have open windows and greater circulation of air than is common.

Some have gone so far as to place exercise over against temperance in eating, saying that if you take enough exercise you may eat and drink what you please. While there is some truth in this there is really no antagonism between them; in fact, they are usually found together.

Another view almost universally advocated, is to avoid drugs. The importance of this and its union with right exercise have been demonstrated in the impressive language of fable.

"There is a story in the 'Arabian Nights' Tales'," says Addison, "of a king who had long languished under an ill habit of body, and had taken abundance of remedies to no purpose. At length, says the fable, a physician cured him by the following method: he took a hollow ball of wood, and filled it with several drugs; after which he closed it up so carefully that nothing appeared. He likewise took a mallet, and, after having hollowed the handle and that part which strikes the ball, he inclosed in them several drugs after the same manner as in the ball itself. He then ordered the sultan, who was his patient, to exercise himself early in the morning with these rightly prepared instruments, till such time as he should sweat; when, as the story goes, the virtue of the medicaments perspiring through the wood, had so good an influence on the sultan's constitution, that they cured him of an indisposition which all the compositions he had taken inwardly had not been able to remove.

"This Eastern allegory is finely contrived to show us how beneficial bodily labor is to health, and that exercise is the most effectual physic."

Another illustration is furnished us by Sir William Temple:—

"I know not," he says, "whether some desperate degrees of abstinence would not have the same effect upon other men, as they had upon Atticus; who, weary of his life as well as his physicians by long and cruel pains of a dropsical gout, and despairing of any cure, resolved by degrees to starve himself to death; and went so far, that the physicians found he had ended his disease instead of his life."

Of all the methods advocated, possibly one of the most universally recognized is joyousness,—a hopeful attitude toward life, a cheerful, kindly relationship with one's kind.

According to Galen, Æsculapius wrote comic songs to promote circulation in his patients.

"A physician," says Hippocrates, "should have a certain ready wit, for sadness hinders both the well and the sick."

We know, too, that Apollo was not only the god of music and poetry but also of medicine. The poet, John Armstrong, has explained this:

"Music exalts each joy, allays each grief,
Expels disease, softens every pain;
And hence the wise of Ancient days adored
One power of physic, melody and song."

Sir Charles Clark, one of the greatest physicians of modern times, exercised a most exhilarating influence over his patients by his cheerfulness and jollity. It was probably one of the chief means of his wonderful success.

"Cheerfulness," says Sir John Byles, "is eminently conducive to health both in body and mind."

A recent writer says of Professor Charles Eliot Norton that he was "not of a rugged constitution, yet he did an enormous amount of work and lived to a beautiful old age." This is attributed to the fact that he was never "blue." The cheerful kindliness of his face, his genial smile and kind words were sources of great inspiration to me when a teacher at Harvard, and to all who met him.

The more we investigate the theories of long life the more do we become impressed with a universal longing for a length of days. We find a deep, underlying instinct "that men do not live out half their days." Everywhere, too, we find a certain expectation of "finding the fountain of youth," a hope in some way to conquer sickness and death.

This desire is normal and natural. It may, sometime in future history, be realized.

As we examine these theories we find, however wild they may seem at first, certain common sense views at the heart of all of them. No one need make a hobby of any one of them. Temperance, regularity, repose, patience, and above all, cheerfulness, do not exclude each other, they rather imply one another. In many instances one can hardly be practiced without some of the others. The practice of one would unconsciously bring up the others.

If we study carefully these theories, and especially if we study the lives of those who have not only professed theories but have faithfully practiced their principles and attained great health and age, we always find a combination of various methods.

There is no doubt, for example, that Cornaro completely reformed his life.

The character of Socrates was the secret of his good health. Temperance to the Greek did not mean total abstinence. It meant lack of extravagance; it meant what we mean by patience, by an unruffled temper,—it meant the right use of all the faculties and powers.

What new hobby, you may ask, is the theme of this book? Nothing that will interfere with the fundamental elements of the best ideas of all ages. First of all it is advocated that we go down deeper into all theories. Temperance should not be applied merely to food and drink but must cover self-control, repose of life, purity and depth of thought, and a harmonious development of human nature. The book tries to draw attention to many important things which are usually overlooked or not considered necessary to health and life.

The study of expression, to choose only one example, reveals to us, the necessity of a right poise of the body. One of the leading teachers of science in this country, after fighting tuberculosis for three years, changing climates and using all the help that science has provided, determined at last to go back to his work and to do his best even though he lost his life.

Making a constant and careful study of himself he again began his life as a teacher. He met with one with great knowledge of the human body, one who had studied it from many points of view. He was surprised when that expert said to him:—"Your dieting will not do you much good, that is not your trouble. You do not sit right nor stand right, your chest is too low, it not only cramps your breathing but what is still more important, it cramps your stomach and all the other vital organs." The scientist eagerly asked what he could do to recover his strength, and he received a few valuable suggestions, which he followed, and in six months he was stronger than ever.

As a student and teacher of human expression for nearly forty years, I have found most important connections between man's mind, body and voice. The right use of the voice is next to impossible unless a man stands properly. There are certain inter-relations between the simple conditions and actions of the body, and the conditions and the true use of the voice are determined by the way a man thinks and feels.

A man must not only have right feeling but must express it. He cannot get right expression without right thinking. Health, itself, is one of man's mental and emotional conditions.

This book is an endeavor to study human unfoldment from an all-sided observation of the whole nature of man. Man is a unity, and an endeavor to establish health from a mere material point of view has always failed. Expression is a study from a higher point of view. The organism is studied from the point of view of its mental function. Expression implies the subordination of the body to the actions of the mind. This gives a truer point of view for an all-sided human development.

It also implies a study of the especial significance and use of certain primary acts of our lives:—such as the way we wake up in the morning and certain movements which are taken at that time by animals and normal beings. The stretches, yawnings and breathings, peculiar to that moment, are never lost by animals, but human beings, with their higher possibilities but greater power of perversion, lose the significance and helpfulness of this primarily instinctive movement.

The study of expression also reveals to us that certain emotions are normal or positive and develop health and strength, while certain other emotions are negative and destructive of vitality as well as of manhood. We also find that the emotions we choose to express become our own and, therefore, we should choose normal conditions of mind and emotions, and express these consciously and deliberately, especially at the most negative time in the morning, when we first wake up.

Expression is one of the necessary elements of human development. We control emotions and control their expression. We welcome noble thoughts or noble feelings, and that which we welcome we become.

This book shows the smile, laughter, the taking of breath and the simple stretch as most important exercises which are to be regularly taken. It also implies a deeper study into human co-ordinations; it tries to show a universal necessity of rhythm and is an endeavor to establish the higher principles of training in a way that makes them applicable to the most simple of human actions.

The student is requested to study himself, to make a demonstration of every claim and of more than is claimed. The exercises are so simple that anyone can try and prove them, only let the trial be one continued long enough to be a real test.

The moment you awake center attention upon a pleasant thought or take an attitude of joy, thanksgiving and love for all the world. Have courage and confidence that all evils will vanish; express some normal feelings at once by the expansion of the chest, a deep full breath, an inward laugh or chuckle and an increased harmonious stretch of the whole body.

Everyone will be tempted to say that he cannot control his thoughts. He may say he does not wish to be a hypocrite and try to excuse himself for brooding over gloomy thoughts or the fear that he will not get through the day. Such lack of courage, lack of faith, lack of thanks for the beauties of life are sins which cannot be too strongly condemned.

We can and must at once put ourselves in a positive attitude of mind. We must begin our day with a song, with a smile. We must look upward, not downward. We must reject every discordant thought and accept accordant ones regarding the coming day. It is a new day which brings new life, new joys, new duties, it may be new trials, but these, instead of being accepted as obstacles, may be turned into opportunities.

The indulgence of negative thoughts in the morning may become a habit. A great battle may have to be fought at first, but perseverance and promptness can correct such evil tendencies. It is at this time that the demon of regret and of disappointment is apt to lay hold of us; the blackest thought in our lives likely to meet us.

Observe that this was so of Pippa. Though she awoke with joy, and is held up as an ideal, as she goes on thinking the darkest shadow of her life comes to her.

"If I only knew
What was my mother's face—my father, too!"

This thought, however, she puts out of her mind by resolution, by turning, as we always should turn at such an hour, to the Source.

"Nay, if you come to that, best love of all
Is God's; then why not have God's love befall
Myself as, in the palace by the Dome,
Monsignor?—who to-night will bless the home
Of his dead brother."

Here must begin the heroic endeavor to live. Effort will be required for a time till the habit is formed.

Instantly control the attention and express it by action. Give a positive welcome to the day and the light; express positive thanksgiving for the thought that you have strength and that you have the joy of work to do.

It is in the morning that we should begin to live a new life, a simple life; it is then that we should eliminate all whines and abnormal desires and open our hearts to receive the strength of a new day.

Life, growth and development respond to joy. Every flower seems to smile to meet the sun, and the little bird sings in the midst of its duties.

Some scientists are hoping to discover the germ of old age, and by destroying this to prolong life. The real germ, however, of old age is found in the doubt and worry which we allow to enter the holy of holies of the heart at the holiest hour of the day. If we guard the sacred shrine of thought and consciousness from impure, unkind and discouraging ideas at the moment of awaking it may be truly said that the enjoyments of life as well as its length will be doubled.

The primary acts that express this joy are: first, expansion; second, taking a deep breath; third, stretching of the body; fourth, a smile or inward laugh.

Sometimes these take place so rapidly as to seem to be simultaneous, but close examination will reveal a sequence, though rapid.

As in life we have to live a truth to know or understand it, so an act of expression embodies the emotion.

True enjoyment is also always expansive. Anger and negative emotions cause constrictions, while joy and love increase expansion.

"As a man thinketh in his heart, so is he." It is the mind that makes the man. When we reject a negative thought and accept a positive one we begin the real battle of life. Negative emotion, every moment it is expressed becomes stronger, and gradually takes complete possession of us.

Prof. James says that everyone should do something disagreeable every day, but there is great danger in accepting anything as disagreeable. We must not only do something disagreeable, but we must accept and do it as if it were an agreeable thing. This is most important. The attitude toward life makes all the difference.

Another great teacher has said, "When a wrong thought comes in, say, Out of my house, you don't belong here!"

Remember that the field of consciousness is a sacred shrine. From it banish everything that is not full of joy and praise and comfort, that does not give you strength and courage. Do as Pippa did. Do not let the devil take possession, as he is always ready to do at this time.

This battle must be fought at once. There must be no delay. Idea will link itself to idea by the law of association of ideas, and we shall soon form a habit of negative thoughts in the morning.

The great point to note is that we should live rational lives, that we should give our attention and apply our own scientific knowledge and reason to the every-day duties of life, and not disregard the duty we owe to ourselves.

Men are continually doing something which they know to be wrong. They indulge in thoughts which they know will poison their minds and characters. They eat food which they know is not good for them. They pour into their stomachs stimulants which they know will dull their higher faculties and powers.

Some tell us that life is a continuous battle. It may be looked at in that way, but if we look at it from a more rational point of view it is a continual reaching up for higher enjoyment. Every day and every hour we must be on our guard; our theories must be a rule of life to be really obeyed and lived. Therefore, to apply our own knowledge to the restoration or maintenance of life demands that we avoid that which is injurious, and that we joyously, gladly accept that which is helpful.

Life is a sacred gift, a privilege, and an opportunity to be enjoyed, it is to be lifted up, and filled with high experiences.

To accomplish all these ends, we should study those moments when we are in greatest danger,—those moments which are most important and when we are best able to control our attention and to command our feelings.

The one supreme hour is the hour of awakening. If we can occupy a few minutes of this time in right thoughts, and right movements scientifically directed and as simple as those of the animals, the effect will be astonishing.

To come down to a few specific things that everyone should practice in order to be stronger, to be more efficient, to enjoy more and to live longer, let us summarize a few general points.

Express joy first with laughter. If you cannot laugh aloud, laugh with an inner chuckle. It is not enough to have joy, it must be actively expressed to have an effect upon the organism.

Maintaining the joy and laughter, express, therefore, all harmonious extensions of the body, that is, all simple stretches. Maintaining the laughter and the extension of the body, expand the chest and torso as much as possible.

On waking up, take a thought of joy, of courage, of love toward all mankind, toward the day and its work.

Maintaining all previous conditions, take a full, deep breath.

Set free with the simplest movements every part of the body.

Co-ordinate the parts of the body concerned in every-day work, and sustain them with primary and normal activities.

Bring all the parts of the body into normal rhythm by alternative activity of the parts and in other ways.

To have good health we must rejoice, laugh, extend, expand, breathe, co-ordinate the primary parts of the body, act rhythmically, set free all the parts of the body and all the primary activities of function.

In short, this book tries to move everyone to study the simplest things, the simplest actions, the most normal duties of a human being, and to assert these and to exercise them the very first thing in the morning.

III.
WHAT IS AN EXERCISE?

On account of the many misconceptions of the nature of human development, will it not be well, before beginning our program to consider seriously—What is training? What are some of its principles? What can we do with ourselves by obeying nature's laws? Or, if these questions are too serious, too difficult for a short answer, should we not, at least, try to realize what is an exercise?

To many persons, any kind of movement, any jerk or chaotic action, is an exercise. They think that the more effort put forth, the better. Thus some teachers of voice contend that, to be an exercise, there must be muscular effort in producing tone. On the contrary, many movements are injurious; unnecessary effort will defeat some of the most important exercises.

The exercise must obey the laws of nature. It must fulfill nature's intentions, stimulate nature's processes, awaken normal, though slumbering activity.

An exercise is of fundamental importance to all human beings. Man comes into the world the feeblest of all animals. He has the least power to do anything for himself, but he comes with possibilities of higher love and union with his fellow-men. He comes into the world with a greater possibility of unfolding than any other created being.

Accordingly an exercise is a means of progress, a simple action which a man must use for his own unfoldment.

An exercise is a conscious step toward an ideal.

Man is given the prophetic power to realize his own possibilities. We can hardly imagine an exercise independent of the conscious sense of the highest and best attainments, of thereby making ourselves stronger and in some way better.

This ideal is instinctive, even on the part of animals, in fact, the animal instinctively regards its own preservation, its own unfoldment and the reaching of its ideal type.

A tree will cover up its wound and reach out its branches freely, spontaneously in the direction of the light and toward the attainment of its own type.

With man the ideal is a matter of higher realization. We have the lower instincts in common with the animals but we have also something higher. There is inborn in us a conception that man transcends all present conditions.

An exercise is a step towards the attainment of a chosen end.

Accordingly we have high exercises and low exercises; exercises on a mental and on a physical plane; exercises that may train men down to an abnormal type; exercises also that are intellectual, imaginative and spiritual.

Everywhere in nature there is a low and a high. In animals of a high order of unfoldment there is specific functioning of every part but in those of a low order the functions are confused. The organs are not so well differentiated.

Even in human beings, in the process of degeneracy a man loses a greater variety of his powers, and his very voice and body lose some of those characteristics which belong to the ideal member of the race.

A true exercise always brings sound and specific parts into action. Part is differentiated from part. All parts are made more flexible and more capable of discharging a function distinct from all other parts of the body. A true action of the hand cannot be performed by the foot nor can a foot become a hand except by a process of degeneracy.

An exercise implies a struggle upward over against a drift downwards.

An exercise is an aspiration.

An exercise is a demonstration, it reveals a man's best to himself. It is a process of translating his dreams into reality. It is the only proof of himself, his intuitive language.

An exercise is not physical but mental.

Never regard your exercises as merely physical. The expression "physical training" is a misnomer. All training is the action of mind. It may manifest itself in a physical direction, but training itself,—the putting forth,—is mental. It is the emotion we feel more than the movement that accomplishes results.

No matter who laughs, consider your morning exercises sacred to you. Make them a part of your very life and habits, and put into them your thought and the attitude of your mind toward your fellow-beings.

You will be tempted to regard such movements as merely mechanical and artificial. You will be tempted to think they are just the ideas of some crank.

Put all this aside. Begin your exercises joyously and happily, for the very pleasure of the action.

Remember that you are not a body in which you have a soul; you are a soul and have a body. The cause of everything, even of health, is in our minds. Our awakening is not a physical matter.

There is no power in the material body to move a finger. An exercise is bringing a mental action into manifestation. However physical an action may appear, its only significance is as an act of mind.

An exercise is an expression.

It is an act of being, not of body; it is activity of being in action of body. There is no such thing as physical expression.

Expression is not merely a reflex action. It is the emanation of activity. It is the union of thinking, feeling and willing.

An exercise implies that we can choose what we are to express. It implies also that we can consciously regulate, guide or accentuate our mental, imaginative and emotional activities.

Here we find the importance also of expression as an educational view. Repression and suppression may be injurious to health. Expression is necessary even for the proper functioning of the vital organs. Impression implies the conscious use of an impulse. It implies the ability to share our ideas, feelings or experiences with others.

An exercise is a means of turning an impulse in a higher direction. It implies also the curbing of abnormal impulses.

Exercise implies stimulation of normal functioning. It is an endeavor, but one in accordance with principle.

Thus, an exercise is an expression of an aspiration. Exercise implies many things. It implies that a man may be low down but that he can rise; it implies that if he begin early and work patiently enough he can control, soon or late, his nature. He can control the expression of his being and every manifestation of life if he will only come close enough to the fountain-head of thinking and feeling. He must be willing to demonstrate on an humble plane, and, while striving for the highest ideal, take the simplest exercise as the first step of the ladder.

An exercise localizes function. Every part of the body, even every muscle has certain functions to discharge. Awkward men use the wrong part to perform a certain action; part interferes with part. A true exercise will train each part to discharge its own function and bring it into harmonious co-ordination with other parts. It will stimulate both growth and development but make growth precede development.

While aspiration is universal it becomes conscious in a human being. We have definite ideals and not only instincts for their attainment, but we can adopt rational methods for their realization. We have not only an instinctive consciousness of what is normal but a deep intuition that we can improve every power of our being, every agent of our body and every tone of the voice.

A simple, a most commonplace action, when done with aspiration becomes an exercise. In fact, everything that man does is part of the training. A true list of exercises must reflect the spirit of all life.

A normal man can distinguish between a wrong and a right exercise, between that which will lift him upward and that which will cause degeneracy. When men give up to their lower appetites they strengthen the downward impulses, but the mind can be awakened and every little step will become a demonstration of higher possibilities. An exercise is a demonstration to a man of his possibilities.

Sometime the science of sciences will be that of training and education.

All over the organic world we find tendencies toward degeneracy or downward; and we find everywhere aspirations or activities upward.

Every bird, every rose, every blade of grass is trying to reach an ideal. This universal upward tendency or process we call by some big words which confuse our minds and obscure the facts.

An exercise is not only mental but emotional, not only expressive of thought but of normal emotion.

The wise doctor looks at his patient. He does this not only to recognize the patient's condition but to see how much courage he has, how much joy, how gladly he accepts life.

An exercise demands accentuation of extension.

Muscles should have a certain normal length and the power of relaxation to take a certain length. On account of abnormal positions, such as obtain during sleep, certain muscles become unduly elongated and others too short. To restore the balance of proper proportions those shortened need extension and the elongated need shortening. Accordingly the so-called extensor muscles of the body need frequent action.

The effect of these stretches is to harmonize the vital forces. When a man lies upon his bed, as has been said, he breathes less, the circulation is more or less impeded; hence, the dull feeling and unwillingness to rise.

The stretch also equalizes the circulation. It affects the veins where the pressure of blood is weakest, where there is a more immediate indication of congestion, so that the bad blood flows away, and the good blood from the arteries where the pressure of blood is strong, flows in, and the processes of life go on with more decision.

There is still another explanation why the stretch is so important. It is primarily activity of the extensor muscles and is vitally connected with all true expansion. The flexor muscles on account of the position in sitting and because of a lack of expansive activity, often become too short. They can be extended only by activity of the extensor muscles. The stretch is the special and instinctive action of the extensor muscles in response to a distinctive demand for freedom of the organs, or harmony of the whole myological mechanism. It is also, as has been said, closely connected with the circulation, and the activity of the vital organs.

There is no more important exercise than stretching. Its neglect is one of the strange things in training. One who wishes to be stronger, to have the normal possession of all his faculties, powers and organs, can be initiated and secure the result most rapidly, by the use of this simple and elemental exercise.

An exercise is an act of expansion.

The action of man's body consists of expansion, contraction and modulation, the latter being the union of the other two.

True energy expresses itself primarily by expansion. Life expands and any increase of new life and all positive emotions cause an increase of expansive activity in the body.

The study of expansion reveals to us the fact that expansion and contraction furnish the many elements of all human action, but that expansion is first, that expansion expresses joy, exhilaration, animation in life, and that contraction, aside from its co-ordination with expansion in causing control in intensity, expresses antagonism, hate, anger, pain. Accordingly this book assigns certain fundamental expansions, which everyone should practice and does practice if he obey his own deep instincts.

Negative emotions, such as fear, despondency, or antagonism, cause contraction and tend to constrict the vital organs.

It can, of course, be seen at once that expansion is due to the activity of the extensor muscles. The stretch is, in the main, an expansion. At any rate, it is always associated, co-ordinated, when properly performed, with expansion.

Moreover, if we observe the action of animals and all true spontaneous actions in a human being, we observe that the activity of expansion begins in the centre of the body. It is at this point that we should initiate our expression. The actions in the middle of the body are more conditional than those in the feet, hands, or limbs, but the awakening of conditions should precede modulation. A certain activity of expansion and diffusion is the very basis of all conditions.

All exercises should naturally begin with expansion. A true exercise means an increase of activity. Moreover, not only does life expand, but all positive emotions, such as joy, love, courage, cause activity of the extensor muscles. These emotions, as is universally known, improve health.

If we observe the structure of the torso, we find that the chest has no prop from below; that the ribs are placed at an angle with the spine, sloping downwards as low as forty-five degrees, while at times they may be lifted seventy-five or eighty degrees or more. The expansion of the chest lifts the ribs.

If we study a skeleton, we see that it must be suspended, that it cannot be propped up.

Man, accordingly, stands and walks primarily on account of the active expansion of his whole chest. He is the one animal that has levitation, as will be shown later.

We find that under the ribs in the torso are all the vital organs. The lungs, the heart, the stomach, all these depend for their normal position, their normal action upon the expansion of the chest.

When a man stands, the tendency for the chest is to sag. There are no bones to elevate it. Man has levitation as well as gravitation, and the expansion and elevation of the chest lie at the basis of all good position in standing, sitting and also walking.

There are certain co-ordinate curves, beautiful, spiral, rhythmic, in a normal and healthy human being. These curves depend upon this expansion of the chest.

All the best gymnastic exercises centre in the development of activity in the muscles concerned in keeping the chest elevated and harmoniously expanded.

When we study the expression of this part, we find that it reveals energy and courage and all the noble, positive emotions of a human being.

A passive chest expresses indifference, inactivity, fear, discouragement, a sense of weakness, unwillingness to awake and rise up to meet emergencies. A sunken chest, accordingly, is an indication of a tendency to disease, simply because it expresses a negative mental state or one favorable to the reception of abnormal conditions.

The expansion of the chest, on the contrary, reveals that happy acceptance of life, that active, energetic determination to control abnormal conditions which will ward off all disease and eliminate all failure.

This expansion of the chest, as we can see, is one of the most elemental actions of expansion of the human being. We shall observe later that this activity is directly concerned with erect posture. All actions in a normal condition co-operate or co-ordinate. This expansion frees the respiratory muscles and all the vital organs, gives man command of the elemental action of his body as a whole; that is, his erectness expresses higher emotions and experiences.

An exercise implies co-ordination.

An organism exists only by virtue of certain co-ordination of parts. Training improves and extends this co-ordination.

Co-ordination is the simultaneous union of many different elements or actions in different parts of the body.

An exercise is rhythmic.

When exercises are performed in obedience to the law of rhythm, better results will follow. Rhythm is a law of man's being. Action and reaction imply a human being doing his little part and then accepting the greater work out of the heart of the universe. Action and reaction, activity and passivity, the giving and the receiving, everything natural is rhythmic. Absence of rhythm is death.

An exercise is simple.

The best exercise is the simplest in its movements. It is not the spectacular actions of an exercise that make it the best. As every exercise is a struggle upward it must necessarily be an emphasis of something elemental and normal.

Any movement is normal when it is part of the discharge of an elemental or distinctive action of any agent or part.

The difference between accidental and elemental needs more discussion. Working upon accidentals secures weak results, perverts and interferes with free function. Working upon elementals brings freedom, power.

IV.
PROGRAM OF EXERCISES

As all training is a reaching upward towards an ideal so an exercise is a single step and the first exercise should be the most primary action. The primary condition of all growth is a certain joyous awakening, an expansive enjoyment of life.

Take a joyous thought and express it in active laughter.

No matter how dull or weary you feel when you first awake, joyously accept the new day. Use the following exercises and actions as you would a cold wet towel on your face or hands. Look on the sunny side at once and laugh. We can possess a feeling only by expressing it; we enter into possession of the day only by using it.

It is easy to look at the light, easy to breathe, easy to stretch, to expand, easy to remember something joyous, easy to smile and easy to laugh.

If your body feels weak and sluggish, and you have great indifference to movement there is all the more reason for promptness. If you will joyously extend your arms, expand, breathe deeply and laugh, you welcome life and joy and give them a chance to take possession of your being and body and you will soon feel courageous instead of gloomy, strong instead of weak, rested instead of weary.

None of these exercises require a great expenditure of vitality. Performed, as many of them are, lying down, however energetically you may do them they will bring little or no weariness. Though the exercises do not require much vitality they should be practiced vigorously to accomplish the best results.

1. PRIMARY EXPANSION AND EXTENSION

> On waking, take a courageous, joyous attitude of mind. Chuckling deeply, actively expand the whole body, take a deep breath and co-ordinate harmoniously as many parts as can be brought into sympathetic activity. Stretch the arms upward and the feet downward as far as possible, and repeat at least twenty times.

An old writer gave dilatation as one of the primary characteristics of life. A certain distention of all parts of the body is the beginning of the renewal of energy and a primary manifestation of life. We must give room to the life forces, feel the diffusion of energy into every part. The sense of constriction, due to lying in a cramped position, can be easily removed by this primary exercise.

The chief elements in this primary distention of the body are found in the stretch and expansion of the torso, in deeper, fuller breathing, in the sense of diffusion of life, in greater satisfaction and in laughter. These elements should be practiced on waking up.

The stretch should be in the nature of an indulgence, an instinctive longing on first awaking, a longing in common with all animals. It ought to be enjoyable and a help to sustain the laughter.

Count one for the active movement, or stretch, two for the staying of the active conditions, three for the gradual release of activity, and four for complete relaxation.

The exercise, as most of the others, should be repeated twenty to twenty-five times, counting four for each of the preceding movements. This will require eighty to one hundred counts. Each of the four actions of the muscles should be carefully distinguished and accentuated.

Counting four in this way for an exercise and for each of the first steps obeys the law of rhythm, accentuates all the elemental actions of the muscles and establishes primary conditions of healthful activity in all the vital organs.

The simultaneous elements or actions in this first exercise are of such importance that it is well to practice each one separately, either before or after the general exercise.

This distinct practice prevents the slighting of any of these elemental conditions, restores harmony and stimulates normal functioning of all organs. In fact, all these actions are really necessary conditions and should be present as elements of all exercises.

The following exercises (2-5) are important, individual accentuations of the essential actions of this general exercise, and the conditions of all exercises.

The student should carefully study his tendencies to omit or slight any one of these elements and accentuate carefully not only every step separately, but observe with especial care the one most needed.

2. INITIATORY EXHILARATION

Sustaining the extension and full breath, laugh heartily, with little or no noise, chuckle to yourself persistently for several minutes. Centre the laughter in the breathing and the torso.

Joy and laughter must be considered the first condition of all exercise. The reasons have been explained. If you are still sceptical, observe and experiment. Everything that is truly scientific can be proved or in some way demonstrated. As this is one of the basic principles of this book and its companion volume, "The Smile," and as joy and laughter are met as the first exercise of our program, it may be well to summarize some of the arguments:

Exercise in laughter sets free the vital organs and brings all parts into harmonious, normal activity, stimulates the circulation, quickens the metabolism of the cells and causes elimination. Each of these topics might receive many pages of discussion.

You will be tempted to omit the practice of the chuckle, but it should be especially emphasized.

It expresses and accentuates the permanent possession of the joyous thought. No other exercise can so stimulate a right attitude toward life, as well as restore the normal condition of the vital organs.

It has also, as have all of these exercises, a beneficial effect upon the voice. In fact, all good exercises tend to improve the voice. This is one of the most important tests of an exercise,—does it affect easily, naturally and normally the vocal organs?

3. HARMONIC EXPANSION

Sustaining laughter and extension, sympathetically and joyously elevate and expand the chest as far as possible.

Feel the breast bone separate farther from the spine, easily and naturally as in the expression of joyous courage.

Expand slowly, sustain the expansion, gradually release, then rest, that is to say, perform the exercise in the same quadruple rhythm of the harmonic extension.

In this exercise you should feel a deepening of the chest chamber.

It is well at first, until you get the exercises correctly, to place one hand at the back, the other on the chest, and in expanding to feel the two hands separate.

This expansion should be sustained for several seconds. The release should follow gradually. There should be a repetition of the expansion; you should feel a sympathetic activity all through the chest and torso.

Sudden collapses should at all times be avoided, and they should especially be avoided in exercises of the chest and of the central organs.

The free, expansive facility of the whole chest is the measure of the health, strength, grace and normal actions of a human being. It is of primary importance.

4. RESPIRATORY ACCENTUATION

> Keeping the body extended, the chest well expanded, take a deep, full breath, hold it a moment and gradually release it, then wait a second without greatly lessening the expansion of the chest

In this exercise be sure to accentuate the four elemental parts of an exercise. Taking breath, the active stay of the breath, the gradual release and then the complete surrender of the direct respiratory muscles: that is, accentuate the four steps or elements as in most exercises and avoid the temptation to jerk and to exaggerate minor parts or actions. Constrictions, inharmonious and unrhythmic jerks are always out of place in any exercise. The best results can be obtained only by observance of principles.

Do not force the breath out. Allow it to pass out easily and normally. Increase the inspiration rather than the expiration. The air will tend to pass out too quickly, reserve it and allow it to pass out steadily and regularly.

We find that the taking of breath is associated with the result of expansion and vitally connected with the conception of impressions and expression, and so is a necessary part.

The expanding of the chest causes greater room in the thoracic chamber and breath flows in naturally. This exercise, however, implies that we should consciously and deliberately accentuate expansion and the taking of breath. It aids in the realization of life and the diffusion of activity.

Man breathes over twenty-five thousand times in twenty-four hours. He can get along very well on two or three meals of food and six or eight glasses of water, but with as low as fourteen thousand breaths a day, he is flat on his back and has hardly enough power to move hand or foot.

We live on air. This is one reason why the expansion of the chest is so important. It gives room for breath. In fact, in breathing we do not suck breath into the lungs. Air presses fifteen pounds to the square inch to get into the lungs. Expansion is, therefore, the primary element in breathing. We should, however, at times not only expand fully but consciously draw in breath. We can expand the chest while sustaining it and drink breath into the very depths of our lungs.

Thus the exercise requires us to take as much breath as possible, to retain it a moment, then slowly give it up and at last to relax completely the diaphragm, all the time sustaining the chest expansion. Preserve still the quadruple rhythm. Of course the exercise can be done with dual rhythm, and it will be helpful, but the accentuation of all four of the primary actions will accomplish more than double the beneficial results not only for health but for the voice. It develops the retental action of the breath. A true use of the voice demands a full chest. This exercise strengthens the muscles that reserve the breath and support the tone.

The process of respiration is most directly necessary to all the actions of the human organs. It is an essential part of circulation. The breath we take meets the blood. The blood is carried from the heart through the lungs and back to the heart, then out through every organ of the body and back again to the heart. The whole circulation is a mighty process by which the blood receives sustenance, bears this to every organ of the body and carries back the refuse which is oxidized and given out by the lungs. The blood, according to the earliest tradition, is the life.

All ancient writers on long life "regard the control of the breath as a fundamental sign." A person with little control of his breathing is doomed to a short life.

Nature has so constituted us that at the moment of some excitement, or the reception of some impression, or the instant we try to do something unusual, we take a greater amount of breath. In any exercise, always allow the breathing to act freely. Observe that breathing is the initiatory act or condition of all human effort. It is a sign of the reception of an impression and is thus one of the conditional acts of expression. Breathe deeply and freely at all times. A deliberative breathing exercise, such as the preceding, strengthens all the respiratory muscles and corrects abnormal tendencies.

5. PRIMARY CO-ORDINATION IN LEVITATION

Simultaneously lift and expand the summit of the chest as you actively extend the balls of the feet downwards.

The opposition between the lifting of the chest and extending the balls of the feet takes place in all good positions in standing and walking. This exercise initiates or accentuates the co-ordination of the muscles used in standing. It tends also to harmonize and bring into unity all the conditions so far attained, and gives practical application to those parts of the body which are active all day, in standing, walking and in sitting.

All exercises must be performed rhythmically. There are many elements in rhythm, one is activity and passivity, and another is the alternation of parts:—one limb is active and this helps alternation or rhythm.

6. HARMONIC AND RHYTHMIC EXTENSION

> Lift the chest and extend the right foot downward, then lift the chest with the downward extension of the left foot, rhythmically alternating from one to the other. This is the first step in the development of rhythm.

This alternation is still more akin to the action of the body in standing and walking.

Allow the hip to extend outward on the same side which is being extended.

Co-ordination, that is a simultaneous and sympathetic union of many parts in one action or a harmonious variation of a primary response in many parts, is one of the primary characteristics of the organism. It can be secured by a certain feeling that the whole nature shares in the exercise, that the whole body responds to the whole being of man. It is a direct expression of joy and sympathy. In an involuntary performance there is always less co-ordination than in a sympathetic motion. These are feelings vitally necessary to co-ordination and we must not only have and feel them, we must express them in the body.

The alternation of exercises introduces rhythm, which has been found to be one of the most fundamental elements in training. Rhythm consists of proportion in time. This proportion is in alternation: alternation of activity and passivity, and in alternation of one part with another, as in walking.

Rhythm is the continuity of co-ordinations. Co-ordinations cannot be properly preserved without rhythm nor can there be rhythm without co-ordinations.

The exercises 2 to 6 should all be included in No. 1. They should also be individually practiced in order to accomplish the best results and to avoid the omission of any of these primary elements which should be present in and co-ordinate every true exercise.

After being practiced individually, exercise No. 1 should be practiced several times with a greater co-ordinating union of all the elements. The feeling of satisfaction and joy should be realized at once.

7. CO-ORDINATION OF PRIMARY CONDITIONS

Repeat Exercise No. 1; stretch first the right arm and also the leg, bend the left arm and left leg and so on in alternation. Preserve all the movements.

The difference between this exercise and No. 1 is the stretching of each side in alternation. The same elements should be included.

8. PRIMARY CO-ORDINATE VOICE CONDITIONS

Sustaining all the foregoing conditions; extension, expansion and diffusion of feeling, the retention of the breath and the simultaneous openness and relaxation of the throat, laugh low but heartily:—ha ha, he he, etc.

The tone should be soft and pure. The softer the better. If there is any danger of waking or disturbing someone the exercise should not be omitted but practiced softly.

Joy must not only be felt, it must be expressed. This series of exercises is based upon the fact that the greatest exercises are expressive movements. The smile on the face and active laughter should be used as direct exercises, not only for the body but also for the voice.

This exercise implies some understanding of the fundamental elements of vocal training. The primary co-ordination of voice conditions, that is, the sympathetic, harmonious and elastic retention of the breath causing the co-ordinate passivity at the throat has been explained in "Mind and Voice." This was my discovery and the mastery of it has helped thousands out of ministerial sore throats and other abnormal conditions, and, to my mind, is proved as a fundamental principle. It is of the utmost importance that this little exercise should be practiced in accordance with the principle. The great point of the exercise is the elastic, sympathetic retention of the greatest possible amount of breath and the simultaneous passivity and openness of the throat. The study of laughter or the best possible tone anyone can make will enable him to realize this deep but simple principle.

The effect of this exercise is to centre the breath and to harmonize the activities of the whole man. The central organs should always be exercised before the organs of the surface. The laughter must be sincere, genuine, hearty and natural.

No one can imagine what wonderful effects can be brought to the voice by such simple exercises as these. The voice is an index, not only to mental and emotional conditions but to health. The voice cannot improve truly without improving health.

We reserve breath and have a certain sympathetic fullness due to retention of the breath in the middle of the body. Simultaneously there is an openness of the whole throat and tone passage. All the organs of voice are thus brought into right conditions. When this condition is violated there is a misuse of the voice.

Vocal training consists in the use of such simple exercises as will establish all these conditions that have been mentioned, especially the last. The conditions of voice must be co-ordinated, the vocal organs must respond to thinking and feeling. We cannot ignore, we must demonstrate on every plane. Man is given the greatest opportunity for progress. It is an opportunity he must take. There is no growth, no advance without labor. The labor may not be voluntary, it may not be hard, but man has his work to do. It is a joyous work. Man has an instinctive desire for right exercise which will enable him to really unfold his faculties and demonstrate his powers.

9. FREEDOM OF VITAL ORGANS

> Lying as before, placing both hands flat upon the stomach, keeping the body extended and expanded, breathing full and free, manipulate in a circular, triple rhythm or backward and forward, in dual rhythm, all the vital organs. The thumbs may be placed up under the floating ribs.

This exercise is usually given first in Swedish medical gymnastics. It is especially for the stomach, though it has a vital action upon the liver and other organs. Such manipulations are beneficial to a dyspeptic or to one suffering from congestion of the liver, or from constipation. It is a very important exercise and stimulates all the parts so that they will receive more benefit from the following exercises.

When any particular part, such as the stomach or liver, is found a little tender or sore, special attention should be given to this spot.

10. FREEDOM OF THE TORSO

Preserving primary conditions, turn the hips vigorously as far as possible one way and then the other.

This gives a vigorous twist through the centre of the body. It affects the stomach, liver and all the vital organs, and if the chest is kept expanded and a full breath is retained, it greatly affects the diaphragm and action of the respiratory muscles.

These movements may be taken also with dual and with quadruple rhythm. If done slowly and steadily, in true rhythm and sequence, they will accomplish surprising results, and bring about a deep harmony. If there is congestion the exercise should be performed twenty or twenty-five times.

This exercise frees the torso and makes it flexible. It strengthens the diaphragm and, obeying one of the fundamental laws, exercises the central muscles of the body.

Do not give sudden jerks or sudden collapses, but steadily, definitely and vigorously pivot the hip.

In many people, there are tendencies to congestion in the stomach, and in the neck and throat. This rotary action tends to remove these constrictions and to develop a certain flexibility in the whole torso.

11. FREEDOM OF NECK AND THROAT

Knead with both hands the whole throat and neck, moving every part and eliminating any soreness or stiffness.

The night gown should be unbuttoned and the breast bare. The fingers should be used and also the palm of the hand and the thumb so that every part of the neck and throat shall be set free.

In most persons spots will be found that have some tenderness or soreness, especially if there is any cold or sore throat, and these parts should receive careful attention and manipulation, which should be continued until the soreness is removed. Persevere until the whole throat feels perfectly free and relaxed. It is often the case that some gland is weak and can be strengthened by this massage.

This exercise and that of the manipulation of the stomach, as well as the exercises which follow, have a wonderful effect upon the voice.

12. FREEDOM OF NECK AND HEAD

> Pivot the head as far as possible to the right and then as far as possible to the left.

This exercise is also best practiced in quadruple rhythm. The hands may be around the back of the neck. Knead deeply and remove any congestion.

The efficiency of this exercise may be increased by placing the hands on the neck so that at the moment of extreme pivot the hand may knead the parts. This action of the hand increases the effect and tends, in cases of congestion around the throat or ears, to give great assistance towards the elimination of all abnormal conditions. The other exercises for the manipulation of the throat tend to correct catarrhal conditions.

13. ELEVATION AND EXTENSION OF LOWER LIMBS

> Observing all the conditions, lift the right foot, knee straight, as high as possible, then slowly release it, then lift the left in the same way.

The movement should also be done in quadruple rhythm. The lift should be slow, and there should be a decided staying of the activity, and then a very slow release; then complete rest.

The effect of this exercise is to accentuate further the idea of rhythm; that is, it requires alternate activity and passivity in sequence or a continuity of co-ordinations.

In performing this exercise almost an ache may be felt at the back of the legs, especially at the back of the knees. This is due to the fact that these muscles become too short in sitting and therefore need extension. This exercise gives extension to these muscles. Similar aches will always indicate a lack of extension and call for special help and practice of the opposing muscles.

Of course, it can be seen that whenever parts of the body, such as the knees, are kept bent, the muscles at the front of the limb will grow too long and those at the back of it, too short. Hence, when a man stands up there is a tendency to stand with the knee bent. Old men have a lack of firm backward spring in the knee. It is the aim of several of the exercises to cure this.

14. EXTENSION OF THE BACK

With the body well expanded, kept straight, breathing free and full, lift the hips bearing the weight upon the back of the shoulders and the heel.

This exercise needs to be practiced with quadruple rhythm slowly. It gives wonderful exercise to the central muscles and organs of the torso.

15. ELEVATION OF LOWER LIMBS

With the body well extended and all conditions sustained, lift both legs, knees straight, hold, slowly release, then completely rest.

This exercise is the best help that can be given for a hollow back. It also brings activity into all the abdominal muscles. It will strengthen the muscles concerned in the support of the voice. If the chest is kept well expanded and the lungs full of breath, the exercise will have a wonderful effect upon the diaphragm and the respiratory mechanism. It will strengthen and deepen the breathing and make it more central and reposeful.

16. RHYTHMIC ALTERNATION IN EXTENSION

Combine the last two exercises and give them in alternation. First, lift the body, then rest, then lift both feet, then the body, and so on.

This alternate movement will bring great relief. The muscles are more or less opposed; at any rate, the activity concerned in each exercise will receive a rest during the other action.

This, of course, uses rhythm as an aid. True, natural rhythm is always helpful and should be introduced whenever possible.

17. ROTARY ACTION OF THE FEET

With the heels resting upon the bed carry the balls of the feet in the widest possible circle.

This exercise may be omitted, but it is very important for one who is lacking in freedom in the feet or who suffers from cold feet. It also brings into action the lower extremities and tends to further equalize the circulation.

18. MOBILITY OF THE FACE

> Rest a moment and feel a sense of satisfaction and then smile and place both hands upon the face, covering it as far as possible and knead the muscles, so as to eliminate every constriction and allow the diffusion of the smile to go into every part.

Do not laugh at this exercise but observe the effect. This exercise, however, should be practiced in union with the smile.

Pay especial attention to any part of the face where there are constrictions or tendencies to constriction, and especially any part that may seem to droop.

Where there has been a good deal of suffering or whining, or both, certain parts of the face, especially the corners of the mouth, are turned downward. This habitual action causes the muscles that lift the corners of the mouth to become too long while the corresponding muscles that draw the mouth down become abnormally short. Kneading is, primarily, to give extension to the muscles that have become too short, and the laughter at the same time is to give exercise to the muscles that have become too extended or elongated.

All parts of the face will be brought into proportion. Crows' feet will be eliminated and the beauty and expression of the countenance greatly increased. Where there seems to be no muscle between the skin and bone, as sometimes in the forehead, there must be manipulation, exercise of the weak muscles.

In the case of the face we have to bring in so-called secondary motions. We have to use the hands in the way indicated to get any effect. Of course, the effect will be temporary unless the disposition is changed. The mental and emotional actions are always the primary cause, but frequently the condition of the muscles has become such that it will take a long time to effect a change. The exercises, accordingly, are a wonderful help.

If one-tenth of the power of this exercise to help the countenance were realized, it would not be neglected.

One of my students opened a room and secured quite a following in facial massage by using these exercises. Some cruder than this one were used, though good results were accomplished. This exercise, as here suggested, can be done by anyone alone. If people use it who have constricted countenances, they should carefully emphasize the smile. That has not been done and hence the best results have not been secured.

The faithful practice of such an exercise and especially the study of the significance of the smile and the practice of laughter, in union with other exercises for the stimulation of vitality, will work wonders in the expressive mobility and beauty of the countenance.

It is worth ten times all the cosmetics as a beautifier. It would banish "Beauty Parlors." It is not, however, for the restoration of beauty of the countenance, but to bring blood into parts that are not used. It has good effect upon catarrh, headaches and neuralgia.

While resting the larger muscles of the body these two important exercises may be introduced, or they may be introduced as the last of the first series, while lying on the back.

19. FREEDOM OF THE SCALP

> Placing the hands upon the head move the whole scalp freely and easily in all directions.

This is really the only effective remedy for imperfection at the roots of the hair, falling hair, or baldness. It will cause natural and rich growth of hair.

It is well, also, to pull the hair. One specialist gives this as the only remedy to prevent it from falling out. Not only will such exercises improve the hair by improving the circulation around the roots, but it will make the muscles of these parts more flexible.

20. EXTENSION AND FREEDOM OF THE VITAL ORGANS

> Turn over, face downward, with the body well extended, bearing the weight upon the toes and the elbows, with the upper arm vertical, lift the hips and torso till the body is extended in a straight line.

Be sure that the upper arms are vertical and the fore-arms parallel with each other. Try to keep the body as straight as possible and get the sense of extension.

This may seem to be a severe exercise, but it is not dangerous. In fact, more than any other exercise it tends to correct abnormal conditions in the central portions of the body. It allows the vital organs to be suspended from another angle, rests them, and tends to restore all to normal conditions.

This exercise should be performed in quadruple rhythm, steadily, and slowly. Attention should be given to the complete rest at the climax. Practice it a few times at first until the strength is sufficient to repeat it many times.

It is an unusually important exercise in case of any constrictions. It strengthens also certain muscles of the torso which are apt to be neglected.

This making a bridge of the body, supporting it by the upper arms which should be vertical, and the feet which should also be vertical, has a great effect upon all the internal organs of the torso. It affects any sort of displacement and any kind of congestion. The exercises may be practiced slowly, rising and then staying the activity for a little while, and then allowing the body slowly to descend.

Take a good rest as the exercise is rather vigorous for some persons, especially those who have any weakness through the torso. Those whom the exercise taxes are they who especially need it. It should be repeated several times.

21. PIVOTAL ELEVATION OF THE HEAD

> Pivot the head as far as possible to the right, and then lift it backward. Release and carry to the left, and lift it backward as far as possible.

This exercise tends to strengthen the muscles at the back of the neck. It helps the extension of the chest, and strengthens those muscles which hold the head erect.

22. ACTIVITY OF THE ROYAL MUSCLE

> Lift the head as far back as possible, then slowly draw the chin in lifting the back of the head high.

This exercise develops what sculptors call the royal muscle. This muscle is active, causes an erect head and gives a certain dignity to the carriage of the body and is usually associated with a properly expanded body.

Of course, it alone is not sufficient for a dignified carriage because there must be an expanded chest and the whole body must be normally erect. This muscle, however, plays an important part. It is at the summit of the line of gravity and affects not only the carriage of the head but has a sympathetic effect on the chest. When it is strong and vigorous it tends to make the whole body erect and to bring into sympathetic co-ordination all the muscles used in standing.

23. EXTENSION OF HIPS AND ABDOMEN

With the body well extended lift the right foot, knee straight, as far backward and upward as possible. Then release, and lift the left foot in the same way.

This exercise should be used alternately and given a good deal of activity. The heels may be extended or stretched downward as they are lifted. This will give greater extension to the muscles at the back of the leg.

This exercise causes extension of certain muscles which are kept short when sitting. It is also beneficial for the back.

24. ROTATION OF RIGHT SHOULDER

Turn over to the left side. Vigorously rotate the right shoulder, carrying it in as wide a circle as possible.

This rotary action of the shoulders may be repeated several times in different positions of the body.

The exercise is important for the freeing of the whole torso. The shoulders of most people are rather weak. They should be strong and vigorous especially in brain workers because their action tends to affect the circulation of the blood toward the head. It has also an effect upon the summit of the lungs and certain regions which need freedom.

The rotary action of the shoulders may be given best when lying on the side. The action of the shoulders, however, should not be neglected as it brings a harmonious circulation in the region of the throat. The exercise tends also to affect the whole summit of the chest.

The active shoulder expresses animation and ardor in passion. A good strong shoulder is also an indication of vitality.

The circular and rotary action of the shoulders, the feet, and the hips, is best performed with triple rhythm,—first, upward and forward; second, backward; third, release. The release may be quick and firm.

Triple rhythm has a very sympathetic and stimulating effect. The run is more of a triple rhythm, while the walk is dual. All forms of rhythm, all of the metres should be introduced into the various exercises.

25. ROTATION OF LEFT SHOULDER

Turn over to the right side, and rotate the left shoulder in the same way.

Whenever an exercise is taken for one side it should also be given for the other unless there is special reason for remedying some condition of one-sidedness.

Exercises for the centre of the body should always be given the preference. There should be as far as possible a series of exercises.

Thus far, the exercises are all used lying down. They may be taken in bed but, of course, it would be better if the bed were firm and not too soft, not too yielding and as level as possible. The exercises would often be more helpful if taken on the hard floor.

It is better to sleep on a narrow cot as Cornaro did. This prevents our doubling up the body and contracting the vital organs. Everyone should lie down to sleep tall, or long, and as expanded as possible.

Another reason for sleeping on a cot is that there are no hindrances to lifting the arms behind the head in some of the first exercises. If we sleep on a bed, when we exercise, the body should be placed more or less across it so as to give more freedom to the arms, or the arms may be stretched out straight at the side although this is not so good.

26. ELEVATION OF CHEST AND BREATHING

Sit erect, as tall as possible. Expand the chest fully, carry the arms forward, then backward, gripping the hands almost under the shoulders, chest out as far as possible, taking a deep breath. Repeat this rhythmically many times, sustaining as far as possible the expansion of the chest.

It will be observed that there will come naturally a desire to sit up. It may be well before sitting up to turn on the back and rest a moment and feel the enjoyment of the actions that have been in the body. If the exercises have been properly practiced, there will be a sense of ease and satisfaction.

27. PIVOTAL FLEXIBILITY OF CHEST

Sitting as erect as possible with actively expanded chest, pivot the shoulders and upper part of the torso as far as possible, first to the right and then to the left.

This exercise may be performed to advantage with quadruple rhythm.

This movement exercises almost the opposite muscles from Exercise No. 10. It also has the same beneficial results in the extension of the chest, the removal of constrictions or interferences with the diaphragm, and has a beneficial effect also upon the stomach and all the vital organs.

It is an important exercise for strengthening the muscles of breathing and deepening respiration. It should be repeated many times.

28. EXTENSION OF MUSCLES OF THE BACK

> Stand, stretch arms upward as far as possible, then carry them in the widest possible circle. Relax the back and all parts of the body so that the fingers come to the floor or near it. Then return and carry the fingers as far back as possible.

This exercise brings extension into all the muscles of the back. Frequently, it is the best possible exercise to develop the chest since the extension of a muscle also stimulates its right contraction.

The elbows and knees should be kept as straight as possible in this exercise. The wide circle should be made not only in coming down but in going back forward and over backward.

This exercise causes great extension of the muscles. The muscles from the heel all up the back of the legs and even of the arms are affected. Then in getting back the muscles of all the body receive a similar extension.

This action is very helpful for the development of erectness of the body. It also causes alternation of the muscles and has a good effect upon the health.

29. EXTENSION OF MUSCLES AT THE SIDE

> Standing erect carry the hip out over the right foot, surrendering the whole body to the left side. Allow the weight to be carried out over the left foot, the left hip being widely extended.

This exercise tends to get freedom for muscles at the side and the hip so that the hip upon which the person stands will naturally sway out to the side, and the free hip will be surrendered, bringing the body very naturally into its spiral curves.

30. CO-ORDINATION IN STANDING

> Standing erect, expand the chest in opposition to the balls of the feet, and allow the body slowly to be lifted seemingly from the summit of the chest upward. Allow it to return very slowly and steadily and to sink to the heels. Repeat many times.

This exercise should also be practiced upon each foot separately. It establishes right co-ordinations of the body in standing and helps in establishing accordant poise. All the muscles in the body which tend to bring the summit of the chest and the balls of the feet into right co-ordination are brought into sympathetic activity. It is really an important exercise for the development of a correct bearing and posture of the body.

In going upward, be sure that the chest reaches upward and that the body is lifted by a species of levitation.

Keep the body as straight as possible from the heel to the centre of the neck, preserving a sympathetic expansion of the chest at all times.

This exercise acts upon the whole body, tending to bring all parts into normal relationship.

31. EXTENSION OF CHEST

> Placing your hands against the sides of a narrow door way, allow your weight to come forward upon the hands, the knees straight. Take a full breath, then carry the body back by action of the arms.

This presses the shoulders back and causes expansion of the chest, and a deep breath should, of course, be taken. The exercise should be repeated many times.

This exercise, as well as all others, should be practiced where the air is pure.

Observe that this exercise can be made more severe by placing the feet farther back from the door so that the weight of the body will fall more upon the hands. In this case the hands may be lower. They should be placed slightly below the shoulders.

32. HARMONY OF RESPIRATION AND CIRCULATION

> Lift the arms as high as possible and grasp a pole which has been placed so that it can barely be grasped on tiptoe, and let your weight rest upon the hands, and endeavor to touch the floor with

the heels. One can easily have a pole placed upon hooks as high as possible inside a closet.

This exercise frees all the muscles of the back and carries the blood away from the head. It is an exercise especially recommended by Baron Posse for brain workers.

After the exercises take a sponge bath, or if preferred, rub the chest and throat vigorously with a rough cloth with cold water. Some people prefer an entire bath, but getting into very cold water often has a bad effect upon the circulation and breathing. The water should not be too cold at first until one becomes accustomed to the unusual stimulation. Rub till dry and warm. Injury may follow if there is not reaction.

This program may be lengthened or shortened to suit individual needs. Many exercises can be added by each one according to instinct. Some, for example, those turning to the side, except possibly the relaxing of the shoulders, may be shortened. The exercises may be lengthened also by practicing one a longer period of time, making repetitions of a hundred or more. They may be shortened, too, by giving each movement a shorter period.

Each student must study himself and adapt the exercises according to need. Feelings of enjoyment, however, are not a safe guide. We are so apt to let the dull and stupid feeling take possession in the morning and omit the exercises for the day. It takes resolution to perform them but in a few minutes the reward comes in a feeling of satisfaction and rest. The exercises are usually the best means of removing the feeling of dullness. That, indeed, is one of their chief aims. Co-ordinating the performance and the joyous attitude of man will soon cause the exercises to be developed into a habit and one will feel the need of them as much as he feels the need of food.

The exercises demand joy, expansion, extension, stretching, deep breathing, co-ordination of various parts and the specific accentuation of the movements and harmonious as well as rhythmic alternation.

In general, a person can arrange from this program, shorter ones of from five minutes to thirty, according to individual needs.

The principles underlying the exercises should be carefully considered. This will enable students to remember more easily and more correctly to practice the successive exercises.

Moreover, in the practice of the exercises, as has been said, the aim should be always kept in mind. Thus the simplest action may be turned into the most important exercise by being practiced in accordance with principles and for a specific aim.

To aid those who wish a shorter program, one that will not take over ten minutes, the following may serve as a helpful guide.

1. Combine all exercises from one to seven:—laugh, expand the chest, breathe deeply, co-ordinating the balls of the feet with the chest, and stretch. Emphasize all of these exercises. It may be wise to count say six specific, successive steps: 1, the expansion of the chest; 2, deep breathing; 3, laughter; 4, stretch; 5, gradual relaxation; 6, complete release.

One should be sure that each of these elements is practiced correctly. It is wise at first to individualize them until they are normal and then such a combination becomes efficient and may be in fact advisable as a step in progress.

2. Combine exercises nine and ten:—that is, knead the stomach in combination with the pivot of the hips.

3. Exercises eleven and twelve in a similar way combine the kneading of the neck and throat with the pivotal action of the head.

4. Sixteen may be practiced in a way to unite fourteen and fifteen.

5. Eighteen and nineteen may be practiced as one. The movements, however, should be separated and may be alternated by passing from the face to the head.

6. Exercise twenty, as many others, should always be practiced individually and separately.

7. Twenty may be combined, but not so well with eleven and twelve.

8. All the sitting exercises may be omitted or combined with the standing exercises taken before the exercises on the pole.

V.
HOW TO PRACTICE THE EXERCISES

Since exercises are primarily mental it can be seen that it is not merely the movement but the mental and emotional attitude toward that movement, in short, the conditions of its practice, upon which the accomplishment of right results most depend. An exercise performed with a feeling of antagonism, gloom, or perfunctorily without thought, will not accomplish nearly as much as one practiced with sympathy and joy.

Only thinking and feeling will establish the co-ordinations. Mere perfunctory performance of an exercise or a mechanical use of the will may produce certain local effects, and in this way may actually do harm, while the same exercise practiced with a feeling of joy and exhilaration will bring into co-ordination various parts, and, in fact, affect the whole organism. Practice the exercises accordingly for the fun of the thing; laugh, feel a joyous exultation.

Joyous normal emotion acts expansively. The circulation is quickened and the vital organs are stimulated to normal action. Without the awakening or enjoyment of life the vital forces show little response.

If anyone will examine himself in a state of anger he will feel that it is the lower part of his nature that is dominating him. He can realize that his muscles and vital organs are constricted and cramped. Who has not felt a deep feeling of bitterness, almost of poison, after a fit of anger? Who has not felt a certain depression, at times even of sickness, after antagonism or giving up to despondency?

There is also a feeling above negative emotions of certain dormant possibilities, certain affections and a better nature in the background. In all true exercises this sub-conscious, better self should be the very centre of the endeavor.

So universally is true training and even the nature of an exercise misunderstood that it may be well to summarize a few points to secure intelligent practice.

1. Practice with your whole nature.

Do not regard the performance of movements as a mere matter of will. Expression requires a unity of the whole life of our being.

Regard an exercise as a means of bringing all your powers into life and unity. Let practice be a means of demonstrating your own abilities, spontaneous and deliberative activities to yourself.

2. Practice with an ideal in mind.

The accomplishment of an endeavor implies the reaching or attainment of an ideal. Practicing with no end in view accomplishes nothing. The goal must be an ideal.

There is a universal intuition in an ideal man. There is an intuition deep in ourselves of our higher possibilities. The feeling that better things are possible inspires all human endeavor. Movement merely for the sake of movement, mere haphazard practice, without an ideal, accomplishes but little. We want not only an instinctive ideal but we want one which is the result of thought and study.

3. Practice hopefully and joyfully.

That is to say, there should not only be thought and imagination in practice, there should be feeling,—a normal and ideal emotion. The realization of the possibility of attaining an ideal brings joy, hope, courage and confidence.

4. In every exercise feel a sympathetic expansion of the torso.

It is not only necessary to feel joy, we must express it, and the primary expression of joy is expansion.

Expansion is needed not only as one of the exercises; it is more than this. It is a conditional element of all exercise. From first to last, in every movement, feel also a certain expansion of the chest.

5. In every exercise feel exhilaration of the breathing.

Increase of the activity of breathing in direct co-ordination with expansion is a part of the expression, not only of joy but courage, resolution, endeavor and all normal emotions.

Taking a full breath is given as one of the exercises, but here again we have a condition for all exercises. This is the reason why we should give attention to exalted emotion. It will diffuse through the whole body causing expansion and also quickening all the vital functions.

Respiration is the central function of the body. All the vital operations depend upon it. Perfunctory exercises which do not stimulate breathing are useless and injurious.

6. Accentuate the extension of the muscles of the body in all exercises possible.

The kneading of the face helps the parts as well as being important in itself. If we rub the muscles while whining we tend to confirm the condition in the parts at the time. Thus we may develop whines and frowns. It is very important, therefore, that there should be a cheery smile on the face during the manipulation, if the looks are to be improved by the exercise.

In kneading the stomach and the diaphragm if we have a full chest, as in laughter, the manipulation will produce a far better effect upon the diaphragm than if we have little breath.

In practicing an exercise, therefore, it is not only necessary to study which part most needs development or which muscle is weak, but it is just as necessary to notice which muscles need extension.

7. Practice harmoniously.

We should exercise all parts of the body in a similar way. If we exercise, for example, the action of the feet it is well also to practice rotary action of the arms, or at any rate, of the head.

We should see to it that when we practice one part of the body the corresponding part of the body should be equally exercised. We should not give more exercise to one side or part, except when there are congested conditions. We should not give much more to the arms than to the legs unless we have to walk a great deal.

8. Practice in such a way that every movement affects the central parts of the body.

Hence the program takes first the expansion of the chest and breathing and chuckling, also the transverse action of the torso. We should be cautious about performing violent exercises with the arms, or even with the feet, without simultaneous expansion of the torso because this is a central action which is conditional to all proper action of the limbs. Contraction of the torso while working upon the limbs may draw vitality from the vital organs.

Gymnasts, as a class, die early because they are always performing feats. Other dangers are found in the gymnasium, such as practicing exercises perfunctorily, using quick jerks and too heavy and labored movements which affect only the heavy muscles. The absence of rhythm and co-ordination, the presence of too antagonistic movements, the desire to make a show, too much work upon the superficial muscles are also frequent faults.

Another reason for the beginning of the day's exercise with joy is the fact that the positive emotions affect a man in the centre of his body. They are all expressed by sympathy and right expansion of the torso. This is not only central in expression, it is also central in training.

The muscles affecting the more central organs should in every exercise in some sense cause co-ordinate actions in various parts. The expansive action of the chest is one of the chief exercises because it not only frees the vital organs but co-ordinates the normal actions of a man in standing and walking.

Observe that harmony demands that all parts be equally exercised, but unity demands that we begin our exercises at the center. The organic centrality of the whole body is of first importance.

We should not only feel expansion of the chest in all exercises, but we should begin with exercises for the torso rather than with exercises for the limbs. We want to reach the deepest vital organs as a part of all exercises.

Sometimes a man goes into a gymnasium and works for the muscles of the arm, for example, while the muscles of his chest and around his stomach and diaphragm are weak. In this case the central muscles may grow weaker. Exercises, not properly centred, will decrease harmony.

I have found many people with lack of support of the voice and weakness of the diaphragm and the muscles relating to the retention of breath, but I have found very strong muscles in the arms, while the muscles in the center of the body were surprisingly weak.

In following "external measurements" too much attention is often given to the muscles of the limbs that can be measured. It is easy to discover the fact that the lower limbs have more muscular development than the arms, but this is of little consequence compared with the weakness of internal and hidden muscles like the diaphragm.

It cannot be too often emphasized that an organism necessarily is one. The parts sympathize with each other, and the higher the organism the more is this true. The voice expresses the whole being and body, and it not only calls for great activity of the central muscles, such as the diaphragm, but every part of the body seems to share in voice conditions.

A human being with his legs cut off can never sing or speak as well as he could before he lost them.

9. As far as possible, always feel in all the muscles a sympathetic action with certain opposite parts that support or naturally co-operate with these.

Specific exercises must be directed to central and harmonious effects. For example, expanding the chest and extending the balls of the feet downward as far as possible co-ordinates the parts that are used in standing, though in a different way. It gives extension to the parts; and to extend muscles is often the best way to bring activity into them.

Formerly a horse was fed in a high trough in order to make him hold his head high, but no horse carries his head so high or has such a beautiful arch to the neck as the wild horse, that feeds on the ground.

Weak muscles may often be improved by giving them extension. This eliminates constrictions and brings more rhythm or balanced activity in opposition to other muscles or in union with them.

The co-ordination must be felt. When there are co-ordinations there will be a sense of satisfaction in the vital organs. The exercises will not weary. They will not be a strain or tax the strength. They accumulate vitality rather than waste it.

Co-ordination must especially be studied and used consciously and deliberatively with reference to the chest. In the start of every exercise there should be, as has been said before, something of an increase of activity in the chest and the breath.

10. Practice all exercises as rhythmically as possible.

Rhythm and co-ordination are the deepest lessons of life and are necessary to each other. Activity and passivity must alternate in proportion as far as possible in all exercise.

Observe also that the active exertion of an exercise should determine the amount of the reaction. We should go as slowly in the recoil or eccentric contraction as we do in the concentric contraction.

Nature is always rhythmic. Notice the beating of the heart, going on constantly for eighty or a hundred years. It acts and then re-acts. Observe, too, the rhythm of the peristaltic action of the stomach.

An exercise must obey this universal law of nature.

Jerks should never be permitted; but all be easy and gradual. Even the surrender of a movement should be gradual.

The eccentric action which results is more important in many cases than the concentric. For example, in the diaphragm we make voice by an eccentric action of the inspiratory muscles. We take breath by a concentric action of the diaphragm, we give out breath in making voice by eccentric contraction.

Rhythm, therefore, means primarily that there should be a rest after each exercise. If we feel very weary we should especially emphasize this rest. It is lack of this rest that causes strain and weariness and makes a person nervous. The normal effect of the exercises when practiced rhythmically, is to eliminate fatigue, correct nervousness and weakness.

Rhythmic movements accomplish ten times more than unrhythmic ones, even if unrhythmic movements do not produce unhealthy and abnormal results.

Observe that nature always responds to rhythm. The body will respond to rhythm. Let the exercise be taken vigorously and definitely. Let also the reactions or rests be equally definite and decided. Vigor should never lead to constrictions or to great labor.

If we lie on our back and stretch one side and then the other it is easier and we accomplish better results as a rule than we do by stretching both arms and feet simultaneously.

It is hard to explain the sympathetic union of co-ordination and rhythm. I have never found any explanation or even reference to this. Even Dalcroze, who has so many good ideas regarding rhythm, has not grasped the principles of co-ordination of different parts of the body and especially the relation of co-ordination to rhythm.

Awkward people lack both co-ordination and rhythm and the two are vitally connected. By establishing co-ordinations we begin to establish rhythm, and by establishing rhythm we help in the co-ordinations.

The principle of rhythm applies to all our human actions. We should walk rhythmically, and we should stand allowing all the rhythmic curves of the body to have their normal relationship. We shall always have the right rhythmic curves if we have the right centrality and co-ordinations.

One of the greatest effects of music is due to the rhythm. All movements, however, have a rhythm of their own.

11. Use in every exercise, as far as possible, all the primary actions of the muscles.

We can distinguish four actions of the muscles. First, active contraction, shortening of the muscles sometimes called concentric contraction; secondly, we can stay the tension of the muscles at a certain point. This is called static contraction. Third, we can allow the muscle gradually to release its contraction, that is, allow it to slowly lengthen. This is called eccentric contraction. Fourth, we can take the will entirely out of a muscle and allow its complete quiescence.

Rhythm demands the presence of all these actions; and also all these elements in proportion. And in the practice of all exercises it is well to accentuate all four of these elements by counting. In the stretch for the whole body, for example, we can extend the limbs slowly as far as possible, and there will be a contraction of the extensor muscles. Then we can stay the body when stretched to the fullest extent. Then we can gradually release the action of these muscles and then completely rest.

Some of the exercises can be practiced with dual movements, first with activity and then release, but by varying the climactic action for a moment and gradually releasing, that is, by giving these a quadruple rhythm, we can accomplish better results than in the dual.

In dual rhythm we are apt to collapse suddenly after a movement. In fact, it is harder to control the release of the contraction of the muscles than to control the gradual increase of their contraction. This is illustrated in the difficulty of retaining breath. Breath is normally retained by sustaining the activity of the diaphragm, that is, its eccentric contraction. However, the body needs occasionally the complete surrender of muscles, but this should not be too sudden or jerky. The gradual surrender brings greater control and the higher type of development.

When we use what are known as secondary movements, that is, when we use the hands to manipulate the stomach or when somebody else rubs us, we should restfully and completely give up the muscles and manipulate them or let them be manipulated in a state of rest.

At times it may be well to manipulate a muscle when at full tension. When there seems to be a tendency to great constriction it may be well to manipulate a muscle during both contraction and relaxation and to test its relaxation. Again if a muscle does not seem to act as far as possible the opposing one may be found too short and may be manipulated to allow greater extension.

12. Practice thoughtfully.

That is to say, study yourself. Observe your needs. For example, stand against some perfectly straight post or door, with the heels and back of the head against it. Where the back curves most, there will be room for the hand. Now where do you feel the most constriction? Give attention to such parts.

Even when lying on your back, by stretching the limbs and expanding the chest such wrong tendencies or faults in standing can be corrected. The chest can be set free when it is constricted. When it is carried too low you can directly separate the breast-bone from the spine. By sympathetic expansions of the torso and by manipulating with the hands the parts that are especially constricted, curvatures, even in the back, can be improved.

In all cases in practicing expansion we should be careful that there is no increase in the curvature of the spine. The back should remain normal, or become more nearly normal if we find any perversions.

A hollow back, as is well known, is more difficult to correct than a hollow chest, though both of them are abnormal. A hollow back can best be corrected by the lifting of the feet, and the extension of the muscles of the back. If the hand is placed under the back where there is the greatest curvature there will be felt a normal action upon this curve of the spine.

One point which has been discussed is whether training can affect the bones, or only the muscles. The whole body can be affected by training if the right methods are used. In correcting something like a hollow back, which has been of long duration, not only the balance of the muscles but the very articulations and ligaments and even bones may be affected by patient and persevering practice.

If there is congestion in the region of the throat, the pivotal action of the head is important, but the hands can be made to do a great deal of work also during the pivotal actions. Such manipulation is one of the best remedies for sore throat, and also for dizziness, unless the dizziness is caused by a wrong condition of the stomach or liver, in which case the pivotal actions of the torso should be vigorously performed, with kneading by the hands, of the abdomen.

If one limb is weaker than its mate it should be given more practice until balance is restored.

If there is any muscle weak in any part of the body, we should find an exercise to strengthen it harmoniously.

It can hardly be emphasized too often that the central muscles should be stronger than the surface muscles. Whenever we find, for example, a weak diaphragm, we should use a greater number of exercises for it and be careful not to give too much attention to the arm muscles.

It is not mere strength to lift a heavy weight that measures the degree of vitality or indicates length of life, but rather the harmony of all parts working together. The muscles connected with breathing should be stronger in proportion than the superficial muscles of the arms or lower limbs.

People who perform one particular movement a great deal, such as a blacksmith in hammering, should study and use exercises for the parts that are habitually neglected.

A little thought can correct every abnormal condition, even stiff joints and headache. By practicing patiently such tendencies may be practically eliminated.

13. Practice progressively.

Exercises are often taken intemperately. The student begins with enthusiasm, feels uncomfortable results from the extravagance, and then gives up the exercises.

Begin carefully. Patiently practice the movement at first ten or twenty times, counting four with each step and accentuating the stretches, each day increasing a little, and after a week or two the results will be surprising. Let there be regularity even in the increasing of the exercises.

We must take steps slowly, and gradually add others until we have the number which the normal condition of our system demands.

Study your own strength and the effects of the exercises upon you.

There are many ways by which an exercise may be made progressive. First, by gradually increasing the vigor of the movement. For example, lifting the feet from the bed, one foot may be lifted at a time, which is easier, or both may be lifted only a few inches at first. Second, the exercise may be performed more slowly and more vigorously. Third, by repeating the exercise a greater number of times. Fourth, by the addition of a greater number and variety of exercises.

Sometimes a person is lame from practice. This is usually due to the breaking of small, delicate fibres. These fibres may have grown together by monotony of movement and by extending them suddenly or violently they may have been wrenched apart too suddenly. Muscular fibres should move freely. They will do so if we practice gradually, but violent practice may strain unused muscles and thus cause soreness. In general, the actions of muscles should be as varied as possible, but should be easily, progressively developed. Every successive day, exercises should receive a little more vigor until normal conditions are established.

Some kinds of exercises may be omitted at first. We may leave out all the exercises sitting or those lying on the side. A few of the standing exercises may also be omitted.

You will be tempted, however, to omit too much as a rule and then some special day to practice too many. Even if you do get a little sore or lame or feel a little as if you had overdone it is better than under-doing, and nature will soon correct the abnormal condition. The next time you practice the exercise you can eliminate the bad effects of your former practice.

In all cases of sickness, or weakness from any cause, special care must be given to gentle stretches and manipulation. The movements should be slow and steady. Do not leave yourself in a state of pain but of enjoyment.

Remember that growth in nature is slow. The stronger the organism, like the oak, the slower the growth. A weed may grow almost in a night. Be patient, therefore, do not worry,—be persevering and regular in all the habits of life.

Some constitutions need more exercise than others. Those who are growing fleshy need quick, vigorous exercises, while those who are growing thin and emaciated need slow, steady ones, as do those who are nervous.

14. Establish periodicity.

All development in nature proceeds in a regular and continuous sequence. There are certain alternations and variations, but these take place at specific periods.

The organism will adapt itself to regular periods. Thus, if we take our meals regularly, we get hungry at the same time every day. We should go to bed at a regular hour; at that time the system demands rest and we become sleepy.

Parents are so anxious that their children have a good time that they frequently cultivate irregular habits and thus lay the foundation of future failure.

Health is greatly dependent upon regular hours for both work and recreation. Anything that interferes with periodicity in the human body interferes with vital functioning. Observe how regularly we breathe. There is a normal respiration, circulation, and beating of the heart which are practically the same for everyone. Any variation from these regular rhythms is serious.

This principle of periodicity applies to exercises as well as to anything else. Some men have the habit of going to a gymnasium once a week. They take the exercises one day and neglect them for several days, then try to make up for lost time. The exercises in such cases are not enjoyed. They will be performed mechanically, if not perfunctorily: at any rate, satisfactory results will not follow.

If we take exercises every day at about the same time, say upon waking in the morning and on going to bed at night, the system will come to long for them just as the stomach craves food.

Nature does not grow a little one day and then stop for a while; she does not grow a limb on one side and then another on the other side. All growth is continuous.

Of course, this continuity is rhythmic. There is a different action day and night, but this in itself is a form of periodicity. In the same way we have summer and winter. The tree feeds itself in summer and during the winter the life remains hidden at the root while the process of making the texture firm proceeds with rhythmic alternation.

All phases of life and growth are periodic. If, for any reason, there is an unusually severe winter the plants are killed. If there is a long period of drought vegetation dies. A certain normal amount of rain as of air, food, or soil is necessary to the growth of the plant.

One reason for practicing in the early morning is the fact that it will connect exercise with the natural habits of the individual. The time of waking up should be periodic and will be so if we retire regularly. The practice of exercises on first awakening or retiring will also tend to help the normal time and amount of sleep. If we take exercises on first waking, as suggested, we shall awake about the same time and with greater enjoyment.

The system will come to expand naturally; every cell will leap like a dog that prances with joy when it sees its master getting ready to go for a walk.

15. Practice regularly.

Not only should the time be regular, the amount of exercise also should be about the same each day. We should not give a half hour or an hour one day and neglect it entirely the next any more than we should eat one extraordinary meal and then go without anything to eat for two or three days.

The same is true also regarding the kind of exercise. It may be helpful to change some of the exercises, but we should have exercises for all parts of the body. If we substitute one exercise for another we should take care to exercise all the parts equally. We may change the kind of food, but the degree of sustenance it contains should not greatly vary.

16. Practice patiently.

Do not expect great results to come in a day, though you ought to feel some effect very quickly, yet it may take weeks, especially if there is any unusual weakness or abnormal condition. The slower and more varied the practice the better, other things being equal, because conditions are more important than the exercise and the normal adjustment of the various parts of the body is much more important than strengthening any local part.

17. Practice slowly but decidedly and vigorously.

The more slowly an exercise is practiced the deeper the effect. The lifting of the feet very slowly, for example, will have more effect upon the diaphragm than if done quickly. The holding of the chest high while lifting the feet slowly, causes wonderful action of the diaphragm and of the stomach and vital organs.

Slowness, however, does not mean hesitation, indifference, nor laziness. Mere lazy, indifferent practice will accomplish nothing. Let the movements be done slowly but decidedly and definitely.

One should be careful if there is any particular part that causes pain. We should bring in secondary or kneading movements, with the hands. If the action is thoughtfully directed to the right part, if it is truly rhythmic and sympathetic, abnormal conditions will be removed.

18. Exercise as well as sleep in the purest air possible.

Sleep with your windows open. Let the air circulate across your room though not across your bed. Let the air be as pure as that out of doors.

Perform your exercises in bed with your windows open and with but little covering. The vigorous exercises will bring greater warmth and you will feel the desire to throw off the blanket. Some of the exercises, of course, as lifting the legs, cannot be performed so well without removing the covering.

The method of practicing the exercises as well as the amount, number and character of them, depends greatly upon the health and the vitality of the individual, but there must be a continual advance in the vigor and the number of the exercises.

VI.
ACTIONS OF EVERY-DAY LIFE

The benefit of exercises must be tested by the help they give to the actions of every-day life. The human body must perform certain movements which are continually necessary. These exercises enable us to do these movements with more grace and ease, with more pleasure to ourselves, with greater saving of strength and vitality, and in a way to give greater pleasure to others.

1. HOW TO STAND

"Man is the only animal," says Sir William Turner, "with a vertical spine." The bird stands upon two feet but the spine is not vertical. Strictly speaking no animal stands erect except man.

The primary aim of all true exercise for the improvement of health and the prolonging of life must affect the erectness of the human body and the counterpoise curves of the spine. The axis of the spine must be vertical.

Nearly all the exercises from the very first tend to accomplish this result. The expansion of the chest, the pivotal flexing of the torso, the lifting of the feet, the stretching, the co-ordinate action between the summit of the chest and the balls of the feet, and the exercises in sitting and standing, all tend to establish this most important condition.

There must be activity at the summit of the chest. The head and the chest are the first to give up and sag. We can see that the skeleton has no bones below the breast bone to support it. The lower ribs are floating ribs and the other ribs have an angle downward. Everything is arranged with reference to the expansion of the chest. This is the central activity in standing properly.

We can see, as has been shown, that man is held up seemingly from above. Man comes into stable equilibrium only when the body is supported from the summit of the chest. Levitation opposes gravitation.

It will be observed that the first exercises concern the expansion of the chest and when the exercises are properly performed, this expansion of the chest is indirectly sustained through them all.

If we observe a person standing properly, we find that a line dropped through the centre of the ear will fall through the centre of the shoulder, the centre of the hip, and the centre of the arch of the foot. The things that cause bad positions are: the chest inactive, the hips sinking forward, the head hanging downward or lolling to the side, the body sinking to the heel, and weak knees; but all of these seem to be corrected when the chest is properly expanded and elevated.

To stand well, therefore, one should stand upright; the chest well expanded so as to bring all parts into co-ordination and establish a true centrality in the body. In a certain sense, there seems to be an axis of the body by which it rests easily upon one foot while the other leg and hip are perfectly free. The body is also perfectly free to pivot and to pass the weight to the other foot.

The recommendation to "stand tall" is more or less helpful, but there must be some qualification. Stand tall, but not with rigidity or stiffness. The body must be elastically and sympathetically tall, and also sympathetically expanded, man must stand as if held up from above rather than from below, expanded and elevated by feeling and thought rather than by mere will. The centrality, ease and harmony of the poise are of more importance than the tallness.

When one stands properly on one foot a spiral line from the top of the head to the foot is developed. The head inclines slightly toward the side that bears the weight, the torso slightly inclines in opposition and the active lower limb takes a slightly opposite inclination. This line which has been called the line of beauty is very common in nature. It is found all over the human body.

When the face is animated with joy and gentleness, such spiral curves appear in all directions. The presence of this line is an element of a beautiful face and of a graceful body.

The beneficial effects of such a poise are seen at once. The breathing is free. When a person stands in bad poise there is constriction of the respiratory muscles so that he is uneasy, he shifts from foot to foot. But when one stands in stable equilibrium, he stands restfully, easily and gracefully, and can move in any direction freely. His body also becomes expressive and acts under the dominion of feeling.

2. HOW TO WALK

The character of a person's position in standing will determine the character of the walk. If one has learned to stand in stable equilibrium he will walk suggesting repose. If he stand in a discordant poise he will walk in a discordant chaotic way and will be continuously fighting to stand up.

When a person stands in an accordant poise the walk is a progression forward and a levitation upward rhythmically and freely, the spiral lines alternating with every step.

Every line of the body acts rhythmically. There is not only rhythmical alternation of the lower limbs and of the movements of the weight from foot to foot but all the lines of the body alternate rhythmically.

A good walk is the carrying out of a man's purpose. Accordingly there is an attraction forward and upward at the summit of the chest.

There are some abnormal walks where men seem to be drawn by the head, some walk as if drawn by the nose or chin, by the hips or by the knees or even the feet. The gravitation of the body forward toward the carrying out of one's purpose should be from the centre of gravitation and should be upward.

"Onward and upward, true to the line." Man in his very walking seems to be a progressive being. To climb a declivity, he seems to move forward and upward. In a bad walk a man seems drawn downward.

The poise of the body in standing and walking is most affected by this series of exercises. The co-ordination between the summit of the chest and the feet in rhythmic alternation, the simultaneous activity of the chest in all movements or exercises develop good positions in standing and natural actions of the body in walking.

The extensions especially when in alternation bring the body also into the normal spiral lines and tend also to extend the muscles especially at the side so that the shoulder does not seem to be drawn down toward the hip, but acts with the torso freely.

When exercises are practiced properly the whole bearing of the body will begin to improve.

3. HOW TO SIT

Badly as people stand, they sit possibly worse. Most people sit in the most unhealthful as well as in the most ungraceful way. Generally there is a complete "slumping" of the chest, the spine is brought into a wide, single curve instead of its counterpoise curves.

All the exercises from the very first, have a bearing upon the establishment of the normal conditions of the spine. If the exercises are well practiced, especially the elevation and expansion of the chest, the spine is strengthened and its normally proportioned curves are established.

Bad positions in sitting are extremely common. Book-keepers, editors, seamstresses and children in school need careful attention. Special exercises should be given, such as the "harmonious expansion of the chest" in sitting and the use of the arms to develop the uprightness of the torso.

Bad positions in sitting are often due to a false sense of rest. Muscles not acting harmoniously tend to completely collapse. Many people sit without true rest, and are continually shifting their position in a vain search for rest.

What is rest? The chief rest comes through the alternation of activity and passivity, that is, through rhythm. Passivity alternating with activity brings rest to the human heart and is the best mode of rest. Rest also results from normal functioning. A person can sit or stand in true poise, giving freedom to breathing, and be able to rest much more truly than in an unnatural, abnormal, collapsed condition.

This can be well illustrated by the fact that when a person starts out to walk with the chest slumped, the head hung down and with all the vital organs cramped, he comes back more weary than rested.

In walking we should, as has been shown, keep the chest well expanded, the body elevated, co-ordinating all the normal relations of parts. If we walk in this way it tends to rest rather than to weary us.

Therefore stand sympathetically expanded and easily tall. Walk in the same way and sit in the same way. Let there be a certain exhilaration and a sense of satisfaction.

4. HOW TO LIE DOWN

Dr. Lyman Beecher said that one should always assume a horizontal posture in the middle of the day. The heart, he said, had less difficult work to pump the blood horizontally than vertically.

Henry Ward Beecher attributed his power to do a great deal more work than ordinary men to this habit of his life of always resting in the middle of the day.

He justified his habit by quoting from his father, using even his father's antique pronunciation of "poster."

There is no doubt truth in this. To one very active and who performs a great deal of work it brings a variety of positions and greater rhythm. It rests the vital organs. It brings a harmonious repose and relation of parts.

Even in lying down, we find abnormal conditions. Some men cramp and constrict themselves. The chest is allowed to collapse and the whole body tends to be drawn together. Grief or any negative emotion of feeling or condition destructive to health tends to act in this way.

People, therefore, should lie down properly. They should lie down, as has been said, sympathetically and expansively long. They should directly manifest courage rather than shrinking, joy rather than sadness, with thankful animation rather than in a despairing state of mind. By the expression of joy and courage and peaceful repose and with a deep sense of the acceptance and realization of the good of life lying down will mean more. Express this in the body by normal position, by expansion, no matter what attitude the body may occupy. Man, whether he chooses or not, always expresses the state of his mind in the action of his body. And by cultivating the right mood and expressing the right feeling and so exercising the parts of his body as to express normally and more adequately that mood, men will develop not only health, strength and long life; but will also develop a nobler and stronger personality and more heroic and courageous endurance.

The exercises, accordingly, should be applied to the simplest movements of every-day life. They must not be taken as something separate from life, but as an essential part of it, as necessary to life as a smile is to the face.

VII.
WORK AND PLAY

"Blessed," says Carlyle, "is the man who has found his work. Let him seek no other blessing."

A man out of work is one of the saddest of all sights. There possibly is a sadder one, the man who has lost the power to play. The child in whom the spirit of play has been crushed out is saddest of all.

Work is natural. One who does not love to work is greatly to be pitied. Fortunately, such people are rare. When a man finds his work and becomes actively occupied with it he is happy. He, however, often overdoes it and the difficulty is not to work but to play.

Usually it is thought that there is antagonism between work and play. On the contrary, they are more alike than most people think.

According to William Morris, "Art is the spirit of play put into our work." The union of work and play is absolutely necessary to human nature.

By work we generally mean something that comes as a duty, something which we are compelled to do or something which we must do from necessity in order to win a livelihood.

Play is usually regarded as something that is pure enjoyment and spontaneous. A recent cartoon pictured a boy complaining because his mother had asked him to carry a small rug up to the top of the house, then portrayed the same boy, after a ten-mile trudge, climbing a steep hill with a load of golf sticks, the perspiration streaming down his face, saying, "This is fine!"

The same task may therefore be regarded as work or play according to the point of view. The difference is the degree of enjoyment, the attitude or feeling toward the thing to be done.

We can control our attention, we can look for interesting things in almost any effort. In either work or play we require a rhythmic alternation between enjoyment and resolute endeavor.

The principles advocated in this book and its companion, "The Smile," should prepare a man for the work and the play of life. Exercises taken at any time should serve as a remedy for the evil effects of hard work of any kind.

The exercises give the best preparation for work and because many of them are taken lying down they do not exhaust but accumulate energy. They also stimulate and develop a harmony and activity of man's whole being.

The shortest and best answer that can be made to the question "How to work" is, to work rhythmically. This is the way Nature works. There is action and reaction.

The law of rhythm, which has already been explained, must be obeyed in our every-day tasks. It applies to every step we take.

One of the best results of these exercises is that they develop a sense of rhythm.

There are many violations of rhythm. One is continuing along one line too long. Work can be so arranged as to be varied. We can work at one thing several hours and then we can deliberately drop it until the next day and take up some other phase of work.

Without rhythm, work becomes drudgery. A more specific violation of rhythm is a failure to relax and to use force only when needed.

The greatest effect of force comes through action and reaction. Sometimes a man uses unnecessary parts and uses them continually. That, of course, will cause weariness.

There are hundreds of questions regarding such discussions in as many books in our day. Mr. Nathaniel J. Fowler, Jr., in "The Boy," a careful book which is a treasure house of information, has gathered answers to leading questions from two hundred and eighty-three prominent men. Many of these, in fact, most of them, advise a boy, when he is not satisfied with his work and is pretty sure that he is not adapted to it, to change his occupation.

It is a difficult point upon which to give advice, but other things being equal, work should be enjoyed. When not enjoyed there should be a serious study of the man himself, a study of his attitude toward life, a study of his possibilities, a study of his opportunities, and also a study of what he is best fitted for, and an endeavor to find this.

It is surprising, however, how far men can adapt themselves, even change their very nature in accomplishing a work which is laid upon them as a duty. One of the greatest artists of New England took care of his brothers and sisters and his father's farm, at a crisis, and kept a little shed outside the house where he painted at odd moments. He had an avocation as well as a vocation. He gave up his trip to study in Europe as he wished to study; he did a vast amount of work which was regarded by many as drudgery, and he was compelled to study his art only at odd moments. Despite all this, George Fuller became one of the most illustrious and original of American artists. Today his pictures are in all the leading museums, and command a high price.

What is drudgery? Dr. James Freeman Clark defined it as "work without imagination." Anything can be made drudgery. A man can study art, or sing, paint pictures, edit newspapers, or write books and make his work drudgery. Drudgery is working perfunctorily. It is work without aspiration, work without an ideal.

No man can do anything well in life, without an ideal. If a man undertakes a certain work he must begin it by awakening and realizing the importance of that work in the world's life. He must form a definite ideal of the best possible way of doing that work and of its relation to the world.

In short, no man can accomplish anything in a negative, indifferent attitude toward his work. He must look upon it from the side of its importance, the side of its beauty, the side that is interesting to him, the side that shows its influence and helpfulness toward the world.

Play, to the little child—and also to the hard working man—is more serious than work. When work begins to be perfunctory, play is the only remedy. In such a case a man is in a dangerous rut and must adopt a new rhythm.

"All work, and no play, makes Jack," or any other donkey, "a dull boy."

The first principle of play must be to obey our higher impulses. To play means the ability to change our occupation. It means the ability to obey other impulses than perfunctory ones.

Some men regard play as something low. On the contrary, notwithstanding the "recapitulation" theory, play should be a new aspiration, a deeper assertion of freedom, a higher opportunity for suppressed energies.

To play, certain feelings and conceptions of our nature must be awakened. Play reveals character even more than work because it shows the latent impulses of the man. Therefore, if in college, in school, or in childhood, in playing with companions, the right associations are brought to bear, the right persons are received as mates, then the very sympathy and contact with others will cause higher aspirations, deeper enjoyments, more spontaneous endeavor, and renewal of life. Play is sub-conscious, it is giving way in some sense, to instinct; but it is deliberatively giving up. It implies enjoyment but it does not necessarily imply the gratification of low desire.

Something can be said in favor of athletics. A story is told of a gentleman who visited his nephew in a large private school. He went around the athletic field and asked the trainers about his relative. Then the uncle found the boy in his room, digging. He said, "What are you doing here? None of the trainers see anything of you. What is the trouble?" The student answered, "I have been sick and I have been working hard to catch up." "Get out of this," replied the uncle, "I went to preparatory school and to college to find friends, to get enjoyment, to learn how to play, to come in contact with men. That is the serious business of school and college."

There are some who consider this the very worst of heresies. I used to think so myself; but contact with students in colleges and universities has enabled me at least to see the point of view of this gentleman. Many times I have met men who were not getting the most out of their college or university course though you could not tell that from their scholarship or so-called "standing." They lacked the spirit of enjoyment, the power of initiative. They lacked the power of sympathetic touch with other men that makes greatly for success in life.

To my mind there are some games which bring no sympathetic touch among men. Mere games are not always worthy of the name of play. They become drudgery, and they cause certain constrictions. They fetter the whole life. They call for perfect silence, call for the exercise of great mechanical skill. Frequently we find men playing games which are analogous, if not identical, with their work. Games should be different from work. They should bring sympathetic enjoyment. They should bring exultation.

A noted physiologist sent by his government to examine into the physical training of other countries visited a leading school in England and found the pupils one morning, during the best hours of the day, at play. Approaching one of the boys, he asked for the principal, and was conducted very politely to the master. The visitor was greatly impressed by the boys. He asked the principal why it was that his boys were playing during the best part of the day. "Ah," said the principal, "that is part of our method. We want the best time in the day to be devoted to their outdoor exercises and sports. We take the utmost care that the boys shall come into the most sympathetic spirit with each other, and anything that happens wrong on the playground is to us fully as serious as what happens in their studies."

There is a universal conception that play is not serious. Children are allowed to do just as they please. This is a mistake. Froebel has taught the true spirit and importance of play. Some people consider his explanations as being purely speculative, if not insane; but the great majority of those who have really studied child life agree with him.

It is important what games the child is given. The play must be enjoyed. It should awaken creative energy. It should appeal to the imagination and feelings and not be a purely mechanical exercise of will. It is absolutely necessary for the unfoldment of character that the child come into touch with other minds, and also into contact with things.

Someone has summed up the whole principle in a sentence: "Bring such objects before the child as will stimulate spontaneous activity." The objects may be animals, birds, leaves, flowers, balls, sticks, anything which can awaken human faculties or be turned into a tool.

Arts are given us rather for avocations, for our enjoyment, as a test of our ability to appreciate the different points of view. Each art, as I have often tried to say, expresses something that no other art can say, and he is a cultivated human being who can read all the arts and enjoy them. The aim of art is to guide our energies in higher directions, and to stimulate our ideals. Art develops attention and trains us to become interested in a great variety of directions.

As a proof of this observe the great beauty of nature. We are stirred to go out of doors, to go into the woods and note the beautiful scene and the music of the pines that calls us. Nature everywhere seems at play, seems to invite men to come out into her unlimited playground, the playground of universal principles and fullness of life.

The poet, Schiller, explained all art as being derived from the play instinct. It has been said that play is the overflow of life. Life, love, joy, all noble ideals, must awaken spontaneity or they will not grow. All parts of man's nature must have expression and not be repressed. Play is given to stimulate and to express the spontaneous in us, to manifest emotion and imagination and a sense of freedom. Freedom is a necessity of all unfoldment. Even the flower must bloom spontaneously from the energy within. The sun that calls forth the leaves on all the trees does so by warming the roots in the tree and bringing the gentle south winds which fan the waving branches into activity and cause the unfolding buds to be filled with spontaneous life.

The whole world is full of joy and love. It is human ambition and jealousies that bring the hindrances.

The rhythmic alternation and the necessary relation of work and play to each other can be seen in the very constitution of man. Play alone may develop obedience to lower impulses; while work alone tends to repress the higher aspirations and spontaneous energies.

Even a man's health and strength as well as success depend upon the rhythmic alternation of work and play.

While reading over the copy for this book for the last time, when in that agonizing state which some writers know, undecided whether to throw it into the fire or send it to the printers, I read at the suggestion of a friend, Eleanor H. Porter's little book, "Pollyanna." That simple, wholesome story has given me courage. The fundamental lesson in it is that we should find always something about which to be glad, no matter how severe the trial or how disappointing the event.

Goethe gave as rules for a life of culture:—"Every day see some beautiful picture, hear some beautiful piece of music, read some beautiful poem." These might develop culture in a narrow sense, but to broaden and deepen our lives we need every day to see something beautiful in nature, and in the lives and characters of our fellow beings.

Dr. Howard Crosby once remarked that by giving ten minutes to the telegrams of the newspapers any man should be able to keep in touch with the life of mankind.

The Boy Scouts and the Campfire Girls are emphasizing some important phases of education and life which have been too often overlooked.

One of the Boy Scout rules implies that every day a boy should perform some kindly act for others.

The importance of a boy's stepping up to an elderly lady looking for an electric car and giving her assistance, or carrying a lot of bundles for someone cannot be too highly emphasized. These boys take no "tips." They are trained to serve for the sake of the serving. These suggestions and services awaken the higher nature of the boy or girl. Such movements should be universally supported.

One of the most important helps to the boys should not be overlooked. In offering their services they are led to express their best selves. It is important that they should learn to approach strangers with polite confidence and courage when offering assistance.

I gave my seat once to a woman in a street car and at first I felt a little resentful because not by look or word did she express gratitude. As I glanced at the woman, however, I saw that she really desired to thank me but was embarrassed. She did not know how to do so. How few are taught the languages!

If the Boy Scouts and the Campfire Girls do nothing else than to learn to express their willingness to serve they have made a wonderful gain for active, useful and successful lives.

Of course, the primary aim is the good deed, but are not the kind tone, word and polite bow fully as necessary? Are they not the entering wedge and do they not appeal to the higher nature in the same way that the thought of being of service inspires the boy or girl?

While doing is the great thing, yet it is necessary to say in union with doing. There is really no antagonism between expression in kind looks, tones or words, and acts. They are inseparably connected.

These same principles apply also to the Campfire Girls. They must not only be trained to do things but trained to realize their own personalities and to draw out the best in others. Then the actions will begin to be more expressive of the real personality of the boy or the girl and the seeing, doing and becoming will form an organic unity. Someone has said that the great law of education is, first, to know; second, to do; third, to become. The doing implies not only action, but expression. Certainly we do not become what we know till we do or express through word, tone and action.

The most successful men in the world have certain principles to guide their every-day life. If we could only smile instead of frown, when people criticize or condemn us, how much more successful would be our lives!

Every day we can discover something interesting in our fellow-men.

We can learn to listen.

We should work when we work and play when we play. We should not play in a half-hearted way worrying about our work; and when we work we should do so with all our might.

We ought to have regular periods of rest; we ought to avoid unpleasant topics in conversation. Everyone should have a vocation as well as an avocation.

May we not summarize all these suggestions into a few statements which will enable us to co-ordinate work and play, and aid us in our daily lives to obey the principles that should govern us from our first waking moments? Every Day:

1. Smile when tempted to frown; look for and enjoy the best around you.

2. See, hear or read, that is, receive an impression from something beautiful in nature, art, music, poetry, literature or your fellow-men.

3. Think, feel or realize something in the direction of your ideals and in some way unite your dreams with your every-day work and play.

4. Express the best that is in you and awaken others to express the best in them.

5. Serve some fellow-being by listening, by kind word or deed.

6. Share in some of the great movements of the race.

All these refer to an important point—that we should be teachable and should receive right impressions. This is of primary importance. Breathing means the taking of breath. We should begin the day with joyous and glad acceptance of life and all that it brings. A spirit of thankfulness and acceptance is the true spirit of life.

We, however, need active expression. As breathing implies not only taking breath but giving it out, so impression and expression are necessary elements of the rhythm of life.

Hence even these six things are incomplete. We should also exercise our higher faculties and powers, especially those we are not habitually using in our work. Our whole nature should be active if we are truly to live. Our higher faculties should not be regarded as concerned only in mere dreaming. Our ideals should be connected with our daily work and contact with mankind if we are to cease drudging or working without imagination. Accordingly by word, thought or act, we should express every day the best that is in us. Moreover, fully as important as these, we should every day come into sympathetic touch with our fellow-beings and call forth the best in them.

Expression implies a neighbor,—some other being with whom we can communicate. Do not think for a moment that such expression is empty. Of course, we must go on and endeavor every day to serve someone by a kind act, but a kind word must not be despised. How many hearts are over burdened because they lack a sympathetic listener! To be a polite listener is one of the beautiful things in human life. Remember, also, that many who have seen an opportunity and desired to do a kind act have failed from inability to express the wish by word, smile or bow.

Expression is not separate from impression. We must receive our impressions from every source, then we must express to others the best that is in us and become such sympathetic listeners that others will unfold the best in themselves and thus come into that plane where we can sympathetically participate in the lives of others.

VIII.
SIGNIFICANCE OF NIGHT AND SLEEP

Anyone who wishes for improvement in health, strength, grace, ease, or vitality, or, in fact, in anything, must realize especially the significance of the law of rhythm.

Rhythm is a law of the whole universe. The music of the spheres is no fable. Observe, too, the rhythm of the seasons. Everywhere there is a co-ordination of the finite and the infinite, the individual and the universal,—a unity of forces acting in a sequence of natural co-ordinations.

Of all the illustrations of rhythm one of the most important is the alternation of day and night. Every plant awakes and rejoices with the sun and it recognizes the sunset and goes to sleep as the darkness comes. The few exceptions only prove the rule, and even these simply reverse day and night and are equally rhythmic.

The value of day and night to man is well known. When there is a continuous work to be done it has been proven scientifically that those who work at night cannot accomplish so much as those who work by day. The very same man cannot do the same amount and grade of work in a night that he can do in a day.

The human system is built up by various rhythms like that of day and night. There is a natural call for rest, for recuperation and the surrendering of all our voluntary energies that the spontaneous activities may have their turn.

The Psalmist, after he has gone all over the beauties of the world exclaims, "Man goeth forth unto his work and to his labor until the evening." Here he pauses, for the beauties of the evening seem to awe him for a moment into silence, and then he breaks forth into a universal paean of praise: "O, Lord, how manifold are thy works! in wisdom hast thou made them all."

Night is a part of the normal rhythm of nature. Every plant and every bird welcomes night as well as morning.

Serious and abnormal, indeed, is the state of one who cannot sleep. Next to the importance of a right awakening in the morning is the peaceful, restful retirement at night.

Edison boasts of how little sleep he needs, and claims that sometime man will cease to sleep. He says that sleep is only a habit.

As a matter of fact, by working rhythmically through all the hours of the day, by obeying the law of rhythm at all times, a man may possibly need less sleep, but the repose of unconsciousness seems a part of the Creator's economy.

"He giveth His beloved sleep."

By living in obedience to the law of rhythm and especially by taking some rhythmic exercises before lying down, we can sleep better.

Almost innumerable are the suggestions, rules, or recipes on how to go to sleep.

One says, "Keep counting until you fall asleep."

Another says, "Watch a flock of sheep jumping over a fence, counting each one as it jumps."

A third says, "Watch a bird sailing around in the sky. Keep the mind upon it and watch it as it steadily sails until you are asleep."

Someone says, "Repeat the Twenty-third Psalm over and over, the more rhythmic, the better."

Another says, "Think of the sky. Keep the mind upon its expanse."

Still another, "Think of the Infinite and Eternal Source of the universe."

Among all these suggestions we can find some truth. Nearly all of them imply concentration of the mind. If attention can be focused and held at a point, the excited activity of thinking may be stopped and the body consequently brought into a state of acquiescence. They succeed, if they do succeed, because attention is turned from worries to something besides the antagonism, excitements and duties of the day.

Another element in the suggestions is their regularity. Watching the sheep jump over a fence and counting one at a time, for example, affects the breathing and all the vital forces of the body. This causes rhythmic co-ordination of all the elements and the unity of this will, of course, bring sleep. The sense of harmony and rhythm and self-control should be gained; all antagonistic, chaotic and exciting thoughts and all worry should be eliminated as far as possible before lying down. When we lie down, we should turn our attention away from the excitements of the world to something calm and reposeful.

Accordingly there is nothing better than to repeat some of the exercises of the morning. These stretchings, practiced slowly and rhythmically, will equalize the circulation, the taking of deep breaths, very rhythmically, will tend to restore respiratory action and the other exercises will tend to eliminate constriction from local parts.

Observe the necessity once more of harmonious thought and positive emotion, for here again there will be a temptation to dwell upon the failures of the day. It is so hard to forget some unkind word, some failure on our part to grasp a situation at the right time. We can easily remember the wrong word we ourselves spoke and deeply regret our failure to enter into sympathetic touch with someone.

In such an excited frame of mind, with the nerves wrought up at the thought of the day's work and with all these discordant pictures thronging into our consciousness, sleep becomes impossible.

Sometimes one is too weary to go to sleep, or sinks into a deep slumber which is not normal. The taking of breath is short and the giving up of the breath more sudden. This sleep will not be refreshing. Nine times out of ten such a one will wake up in the morning feeling more weary than when he lay down at night. Of course, if a man could sleep for an unusual number of hours, nature might in time restore him. The excitement of our civilization prevents normal conditions and therefore we must aid nature. Man must understand the laws of life and so use them as to find rest properly.

We need harmony in our thoughts, to let them dwell on what is sacred and beautiful that our sleep may be normal and that we may enter into the world of slumber with sympathetic conditions.

We must, also, laughingly throw off negative thoughts and feelings and allow expansion and stretching to equalize the circulation. All the vital functions must be harmonized. As we perform these exercises once more we find various congestions that have resulted from the one-sidedness of our day's work,—congestions around the throat, parts of the body are weary, constricted, and cramped. By stretching ourselves we can harmoniously adjust the activities of our breathing and circulation. All parts can be restored to harmony and we can rest properly.

After all, what is rest? It is not a mere slumping into inactivity. It is allowing the involuntary rhythm of our being, the sympathetic co-ordination of all the forces of our body to act normally. The rhythm of our volitional activities must be given up to the rhythm of the unconscious and involuntary life.

Before this rhythm can reign we must remove all constrictions from any part of the body.

After taking these exercises we should feel the sympathetic enjoyment of all the cells of our bodies, then sleep will be refreshing, the rhythm of breathing will be normal and the circulation and vital processes will proceed easily and rhythmically.

What are the differences in the practicing of exercises in the morning and evening?

In the first place the exercises in the evening should be more steady, more regular, more harmonious, slower and more rhythmic. Every exercise must soothe the excited nerves, the agitated brain, and the weary respiratory muscles, the heart, and all the circulatory system.

Release needs to be especially emphasized. After every stretch, for example, every part of the body must be relaxed. The reaction will take more time on account of the greater activity through the day. We should, therefore, take especial pains to accentuate the recovery or recoil of the muscles into sympathetic passivity and rest.

The object is now not to stimulate as much as in the morning, but to allay all excitement, harmonize the co-ordination of all parts, remove all local activities in the different parts of the body, establish centrality of the vital functioning and the diffusion of blood and feeling into every part.

It is well to practice the exercises on a hard floor before getting into bed.

The more violent exercises should of course be omitted unless there has been a one-sided position during the day. For example, standing exercises will be beneficial for a person who has been sitting all day. We must practice intelligently, and carefully apply such exercises as are needed. Harmony means the removing of constrictions and over-activity in certain parts which one finds upon exercising. These often need to be vigorously exercised so as to restore the harmonious condition.

On lying down on the floor feel in stretching as if the body weighed a ton,—feel the weight of the arms, legs and head.

Often we lie down but soon the excitement of a thought brings us to our feet before we know it. Eliminate all such exciting ideas, then let the stretch reach every part. Let it be slow and steady and let the release be gradual. There should be a complete rest for quite a little period before the next activity. Other things being equal, the activity should be less than one-third of the surrender not only in time but in attention.

Just before going to sleep it is well to practice a few stretches and to give full expansion to the chest and to take a few deep breaths slowly and rhythmically so as to establish a vigorous and normal rhythm, equalize circulation and bring all parts into harmonious freedom.

In order to emphasize the rhythm in our evening exercises we should accentuate and prolong especially the passive rest between the movements. We should not only more gradually give up the actions of the movements, accentuating the static and eccentric contraction, but we should also feel more sense of surrender at the end of each movement. That is, we should feel a sense of weight and of rest at the end of each action, breathing easily, steadily and freely, all the time.

The time of this rest at the end of the exercising should be prolonged more and more especially after we are in bed and have felt the satisfactory feeling all through the body of harmonious diffusion of energy and the removal of constrictions.

This sense of satisfaction through all the body is fundamental and necessary in order to bring healthful and normal sleep.

The harmonious extension of all parts of the body should be emphasized. All stretches are truly conducive to sleep. They allow life to permeate through the whole body. The exercises, before going to sleep, should be less rigorous unless there are constrictions and these should be removed by simultaneous and sympathetic co-ordination of all parts of the body rather than by vigorous movements.

After any local movement the stretch should be renewed and the affirmation made of some thoughtful and beautiful idea—as love, joy, peace. It will be surprising how quickly help will come and weariness disappear. The entire body, in every cell, will be soothed and enjoy sweet repose.

The affirmation of confidence, love, trust, and peace should follow as well as precede the evening exercises. We should make the going to sleep a sacred part of our lives. In giving up our consciousness we should be sure to surrender it to the positive forces of the universe. This is not an idle dream, nor a mere mystical fancy. Even from a psychological point of view the emotion with which we go to sleep is apt to remain with us and get in its good or evil work in the unconscious, involuntary metabolism that takes place in all the cells. We must lie down to rest in peace.

"Dr. Thomas Hyslop, of the West Riding Asylum in England," according to Professor James in "Memories and Portraits," "said last year to the British Medical Association that the best sleep-producing agent which his practice had revealed to him, was prayer. I say this," he added [I am sorry to say here that I must quote from memory], "purely as a medical man. The exercise of prayer, in those who habitually exert it, must be regarded by us doctors as the most adequate and normal of all pacifiers of the mind and calmers of the nerves.

"But in few of us are functions not tied up by the exercise of other functions. Relatively few medical and scientific men, I fancy, can pray. Few can carry on any living commerce with God. Yet many of us are well aware of how much freer and abler our lives would be, were such important forms of energizing not sealed up by the critical atmosphere in which we have been reared. There are in everyone potential forms of activity that actually are shunted out from use. Part of the imperfect vitality under which we labor can thus be easily explained."

Have a few simple sentences full of thanksgiving, of peace and rest. The best are found in the Bible. The words to Moses, "My presence shall go with thee and I will give thee rest," may be given and repeated many times with a realization of their deep meaning and a personal application to the individual.

Not only repeat phrases, lines, and verses, full of beautiful thought, but change these into your own words. Learn to articulate your own convictions and apply them to your own needs,—even paraphrase, for example, such a phrase as "He restoreth my soul" in the twenty-third Psalm. For the word "soul" we can substitute anything according to the specific needs of the hour. We should, however, use nothing that is not in accordance with universal love and the highest spiritual ideals of man and of our conceptions of the universe. We must always remember that truth is universal.

We can change "soul" also to "health," "strength" or "life," to "joy," to "success," to "confidence," to the body or any part of the body which may seem to be afflicted.

There are in this Psalm other good affirmations on going to sleep. Take individual clauses and repeat them many times, such as "I will fear no evil, for Thou art with me."

One of the best affirmations is found in the first of the twenty-seventh Psalm. "The Lord is my light and my salvation. Whom shall I fear? The Lord is the strength of my life. Of whom [or of what] shall I be afraid? One thing have I asked of the Lord, that will I seek after, that I may dwell in the house of the Lord [in a consciousness of His presence] all the days of my life, to behold the beauty of the Lord, and to enquire in his temple [to commune with Him in the sacred temple of my own soul].

"Thou wilt keep him in perfect peace whose mind is stayed on Thee."

Everyone should find his own, should find it in his experience, find it by personal investigation and study of the Bible and through spiritual realization.

We should live in peace with all men, be able to rejoice evermore, "to pray without ceasing"; that is, we should always be in an attitude to receive that which is good and never admit that which is negative;—hate, antagonism or fear,—but we should welcome love and that which we know expresses the "Infinite Presence." Antagonism, hate, discords prevent us from living our hundred years. "Certain classes of men shall not live out half their days."

The last moment before going to sleep should be one of peaceful rest. Say "Not my will but Thine" and give up everything to the Infinite and Eternal.

My own best help is thanksgiving and praise. When I cannot give up the thoughts and conflicts of the day, I can bring my whole being into reposeful rhythm best by expressing thanks that I can be awake and that I have shared in the life of a day. I praise the Infinite Presence that I can know beauty when I see it, that I can understand truth and know that two times three are not seven and that I can participate in the goodness of the universe. Then, before I know it, I have laid aside the conflicts of the day and have passed into peaceful and harmonious rest.

This method of thanksgiving especially applies to those times when I wake up in the middle of the night.

*****

Returning to Pippa, we find her retirement to her own room and her method of going to sleep no less suggestive as an example than her awakening.

She met the first wakening moment with joy and praise as she resolutely put aside the dark thought of her life and went singing all through the day with the same spirit of thanksgiving and love for all mankind.

Now she comes back to her room weary and discouraged, as we nearly all do. She knows nothing of what her songs have accomplished, nothing of the wonderful influence that has been exercised. In her disheartened moment she sees the sunset in the dark cloud and thinking over the day she would like to know what she really has done.

Yet she checks herself and returns to her morning hymn and keeps her faith and trust. "Results belong to the Master, Thou hast no need to measure them." She becomes very humble, willing, and submissive to the hard task of the morrow. Little she dreams of the revelation that will come of the secrets of her own life and family.

"We know not what we shall be." Each of us at the close of life lies down without realizing our relation to the Infinite, without realizing that we are children and heirs. Blessed is he who feels that his hymn is also "True in some sense or other," that life is true and that each one performs some work and it is not for us to say whether it is great or small. They who wrought but one hour received the same wages as they who wrought the whole day.

Deeply symbolical, allegorical, and typical in the poetic sense of human life is Pippa's closing thought as she lies down to sleep.

"Oh what a drear dark close to my poor day!
How could that red sun drop in that black cloud?
Ah, Pippa, morning's rule is moved away,
Dispensed with, never more to be allowed!
Day's turn is over, now arrives the night's.
Oh, lark, be day's apostle
To mavis, merle and throstle,
Bid them their betters jostle
From day and its delights!
But at night, brother howlet, over the woods,
Toll the world to thy chantry;
Sing to the bats' sleek sisterhoods
Full complines with gallantry;
Then, owls and bats,
Cowls and twats,
Monks and nuns, in a cloister's moods,
Adjourn to the oak-stump pantry!

Now, one thing I should like to really know:
How near I ever might approach all these
I only fancied being, this long day:
—Approach, I mean, so as to touch them, so
As to ... in some way ... move them—if you please,
Do good or evil to them some slight way.
For instance, if I wind
Silk to-morrow, my silk may bind
And border Ottima's cloak's hem.
Ah, me, and my important part with them,

This morning's hymn half promised when I rose!
True in some sense or other, I suppose.

God bless me! I can pray no more to-night.
No doubt, some way or other, hymns say right.

All service ranks the same with God,
With God, whose puppets, best and worst:
Are we; there is no last nor first." [She sleeps]

The Morning League of the School of Expression

is a band of the students, graduates and friends of the School of Expression who are trying to keep their faces toward the morning.

If you wish to join, when you wake GET UP OUT OF THE RIGHT SIDE OF THE BED, that is, stretch, expand, breathe deeply and laugh. Fill with joyous thoughts and their active expressions the first minutes of the day.

Note the effect, and consider yourself initiated.

Try as far as possible EVERY DAY to realize the League's

UNFOLDMENT SUGGESTIONS

1. SMILE whenever tempted to frown; look for and enjoy the best around you.
2. THINK, feel or realize something in the direction of your ideals and, in some way, unite your ideals with your every-day work and play.
3. SEE, hear or read, i. e., receive an impression from something beautiful in nature, art, music, poetry, literature or the lives of your fellow-men.
4. EXPRESS the best that is in you and awaken others to express the best in them.
5. SERVE some fellow being by listening, by kind look, tone, word or deed.
6. SHARE in some of the great movements for the betterment of the race.

That is, use your principles of expression to help in such movements as:

1. Expression in Life (text book, "The Smile"); 2. Expression and Health (text book, "How to Add Ten Years to Your Life"); 3. Expression and Education in the Nursery; Mothers' Clubs; 4. Voice in the Home; 5. Reading in the Public Schools; 6. Speaking in High Schools and Colleges; 7. Speaking Clubs; 8. Browning Clubs (text book, "Browning and the Dramatic Monologue"); 9. Dramatic Clubs; 10. Religious Societies; 11. Boy Scouts; 12. Campfire Girls; 13. Peace Movements; 14. Women's Clubs; and

Suffrage Organizations; 15. Reforms; 16. Teachers' Clubs; 17. School of Expression Summer Terms; 18. Preparation for the School of Expression; 19. Home Studies; 20. Advanced Steps of the School of Expression.

Send your name and address with ten nominations for members with $1.50 for the two League text books, "The Smile" and "How to Add Ten Years to Your Life," and you will be recorded a member. One set of books will do for a family, other books at teachers' or introductory prices. There are no fees. The entire net returns from the League books will be devoted to the endowment of the School of Expression, the Home of the League.

Write frankly and freely asking any counsel, and making any suggestions to the President of the League.

Dr. S. S. CURRY, 307 Pierce Bldg.
Copley Square, Boston, Mass.

MORNING LEAGUE QUESTIONS FOR REPORT

Text-books—"The Smile" and "How to Add Ten Years to Your Life"

After a week's exercise for a few minutes either on waking up or on retiring, write out a report of your experiences or answer the following questions. It is not necessary to repeat the questions, simply use figures. These questions follow the first series, published at the close of "The Smile."

22. Do you practice the exercises on waking in the morning?

23. What exercises do you usually take? How long?

24. What are some of the effects of these exercises?

25. How many times do you repeat each exercise?

26. Do you practice exercises in dual, triple, or quadruple rhythm?

27. Can you keep your chest expanded and laugh at the same time?

28. Can you keep your chest fully expanded and pivot the torso?

29. Do you feel great satisfaction after stretching?

30. What constrictions or congestions have you found?

- a. In the region of the stomach
- b. Chest
- c. Neck
- d. Face
- e. Scalp
- f. Back

31. Do you find any special weaknesses?

32. Do you walk with expanded chest?

33. Do you walk rhythmically?

34. Can you keep your chest well expanded during the stretch?

35. Do you practice exercises standing at an open doorway?

36. Have you a pole from which you swing in your closet?

37. Do you sleep well?

38. What exercises do you take on retiring?

39. Do you relax completely in the middle of the day?

40. What chaotic movements have you discovered in your standing? In sitting? In walking? In lying down?

41. Do you breathe through your nose or through your mouth, especially when asleep?

42. Do you sleep with your windows wide open?

43. Can you laugh out a tone?

44. Taking a full breath and laughing, do your feel your throat passive?

45. Can you co-ordinate an open throat and active retention of breath in laughing out a tone?

46. After walking a short distance do you feel exhilaration or depression?

47. Do you use soft gentle tones in every day conversation?

48. When talking to someone who speaks in a high pitch can you act in the opposite way, and speak in your softest tones?

49. Can you make tone as easily as you smile?

For other questions, see "The Smile."

****

philosophic insight, scientific breadth, moral loftiness of tone, and literary felicity of exposition.—William F. Warren, D.D., LL.D., of Boston University.

Lessons in Vocal Expression. The expressive modulations of the voice developed by studying and training the voice and mind in relation to each other. Eighty-six definite problems and progressive steps. By S. S. Curry, Ph.D., Litt.D. $1.25; to teachers, $1.10, postpaid.

It ought to do away with the artificial and mechanical styles of teaching.—Henry W. Smith, A.M., Professor of Elocution, Princeton University.

Through the use of your text-book on vocal expression, I have had the past term much better results and more manifest interest on the subject than ever before.—A. H. Merrill, A.M., late Professor of Elocution, Vanderbilt University.

The subject is handled in a new and original manner, and cannot fail to revolutionize the old elocutionary ideas.—Mail and Empire, Toronto.

It is capital, good sense, and real instruction.—W. E. Huntington, LL.D., Ex-President of Boston University.

Imagination and Dramatic Instinct. Function of the imagination and assimilation in the vocal interpretation of literature and speaking. By S. S. Curry, Litt.D. $1.50; to teachers, $1.20, postpaid.

Dr. Curry well calls the attention of speakers to the processes of thinking in the modulation of the voice. Every one will be benefited by reading his volumes.... Too much stress can hardly be laid on the author's ground principle, that where a method aims to regulate the modulation of the voice by rules, then inconsistencies and lack of organic coherence begin to take the place of that sense of life which lies at the heart of every true product of art. On the contrary, where vocal expression is studied as a manifestation of the processes of thinking, there results the truer energy of the student's powers and the more natural unity of the complex elements of his expression.—Dr. Lyman Abbott, in The Outlook.

Mind and Voice. Principles underlying all phases of Vocal Training. The psychological and physiological conditions of tone production and scientific and artistic methods of developing them. A work of vital importance to every one interested in improving the qualities of the voice and in correcting slovenly speech. 456 pages. By S. S. Curry, Litt. D. $1.50, postpaid. To teachers, $1.25, postpaid.

It is indeed a masterly and stimulating work.—Amos R. Wells, Editor Christian World.

It is a book that will be of immense help to teachers and preachers, and to others who are using their vocal organs continuously. As an educational work on an important theme, the book has a unique value.—Book News Monthly.

There is pleasure and profit in reading what he says.—Evening Post (Chicago).

Fills a real need in the heart and library of every true teacher and student of the development of natural vocal expression.—Western Recorder (Louisville).

Get it and study it and you will never regret it.—Christian Union Herald (Pittsburg).

Foundation of Expression. Fundamentals of a psychological method of training voice, body, and mind and of teaching speaking and reading. 236 problems; 411 choice passages. A thorough and practical text-book for school and college, and for private study. By S. S. Curry, Litt. D. $1.25; to teachers, $1.10, postpaid.

It means the opening of a new door to me by the master of the garden.—Frank Putnam.

Mastery of the subject and wealth of illustration are manifest in all your treatment of the subject. Should prove a treasure to any man who cares for effective public speaking.—Professor L. O. Brastow, Yale.

Adds materially to the author's former contributions to this science and art, to which he is devoting his life most zealously.—Journal of Education.

May be read with profit by all who love literature.—Denis A. McCarthy, Sacred Heart Review.

It gets at the heart of the subject and is the most practical and clearest book on the important steps in expression that I have ever read.—Edith W. Moses.

How splendid it is; it is at once practical in its simplicity and helpfulness and inspiring. Every teacher ought to be grateful for it.—Jane Herendeen, Teacher of Expression in Jamaica Normal School, N. Y.

Best, most complete, and up-to-date.—Alfred Jenkins Shriver, LL.B., Baltimore.

Public speakers and especially the young men and women in high schools, academies, and colleges will find here one of the most helpful and suggestive books by one of the greatest living teachers of the subject, that was ever presented to the public.—John Marshall Barker, Ph.D., Professor in Boston University.

Browning and the Dramatic Monologue. Nature and peculiarities of Browning's poetry. How to understand Browning. The principles involved in rendering the monologue. An introduction to Browning, and to dramatic platform art. By S. S. Curry, Litt. D., $1.25; to teachers, $1.10, postpaid.

It seems to me to attack the central difficulty in understanding and reading Robert Browning's poetry.... It opens a wide door to the greatest poetry of the modern age.—The Rev. John R. Gow, President of the Boston Browning Society.

A book which sheds an entirely new light on Browning and should be read by every student of the great master; indeed, everyone who would be well informed should read this book, which will interest any lover of literature.—Journal of Education.

Spoken English. A method of co-ordinating impression and expression in reading, conversation, and speaking. It contains suggestions on the importance of observation and adequate impression, and nature study, as a basis to adequate expression. The steps are carefully arranged for the awakening of the imagination and dramatic instinct, right feeling, and natural, spontaneous expression. 320 pages. By S. S. Curry, Litt. D., Ph.D. Price, $1.25; to teachers, $1.10, postpaid.

Every page had something that caught my attention. You certainly have grasped the great principle of vocal expression.—Edwin Markham.

Those who aim at excelling in public utterance and address may well possess themselves of this work.—Journal of Education.

The specialist in reading will wish to add it to his book-shelf for permanent reference.—Normal Instructor.

A masterly presentation of ideas and expression as applied in a wide range of excellent selections.—The World's Chronicle.

Little Classics for Oral English. A companion to Spoken English. The problems correspond by sections with Spoken English. The books may be used together or separately. The problems are arranged in the form of questions which the student can answer properly only by rightly rendering the passages. It is a laboratory method for spoken English, to be used by the first year students in High School or the last years of the Grammar School. 384 pages. By S. S. Curry, Litt. D. Price, $1.25; to teachers, $1.10, postpaid.

I am using Little Classics for Oral English in two classes and believe it is the most satisfactory text that I have used. The students seem to be able to get easily the principles from your questions and problems.—Elva M. Forncrook, St. Nor. Sch., Kalamazoo, Mich.

A fine collection of fine things especially suited to young people. Every teacher of reading and English in our secondary schools ought to have the book.—Prof. Lee Emerson Bassett, Leland Stanford University, Cal.

Address: Book Dept., School of Expression, 306 Pierce Bldg., Copley Square, Boston, Mass.

What Students and Graduates Think of the School of Expression

"We know that there is something BIG here. If only we can get it out to the world."—Caroline A. Hardwick (Philosophic Diploma), Instructor in Reading and Speaking, Wellesley College.

"At no other institution is it possible to secure the training one secures at the School of Expression. It is far broader than a mere training for speaking. It is a fundamental training for life."—Florence E. Lutz (Philosophic Diploma), Instructor in Pantomime, New York City.

"The School of Expression taught me how to LIVE. I think its training of the personality is its greatest work."—F. M. Sargent (Dramatic Artist's Diploma).

"I feel deeply indebted to the School for some of the best and most lasting inspiration I have received for my own work as a teacher of my fellow-men."—Luella Clay Carson, Pres. of Mills College.

"The success I have attained in my profession as a reader, I owe directly to the advanced methods of the School of Expression."—Caroline Foye Flanders (Artistic Diploma), Public Reader, Manchester, N. H.

"The School of Expression of Boston is the most thorough and best in the country. It is different from all other schools. I wish I could talk to any who intend taking a course of study.—I would say, Go to the School of Expression and if there is anything in you, they will bring it out; they will teach you to know yourself; they will show you what you are in comparison with what you may become, and they will begin with the cause and start from the bottom."—Hamilton Colman, Member Richard Mansfield Co.

"When I was your student you held before me intellectual and ethical ideals which I am still trying to realize."—Charles L. White, D.D., Ex-President Colby College.

"The same principles of education which have installed manual training in public schools are even more applicable to the training of men's souls to rational self-expression. Dr. Curry will some day be recognized to have been an educational philosopher for having championed principles no less true of the spoken word than of every form of creative self-expression."—Dean Shailer Mathews, University of Chicago.

"The whole world ought to learn about the School of Expression and your discoveries."—Rev. J. Stanley Durkee (Speaker's Diploma), Boston.

Spoken English. A psychological method of developing reading, conversation and speaking. A book for junior students or teachers. 320 pages. $1.25; to teachers, $1.10, postpaid.

Little Classics for Oral English. Companion to Spoken English. Introductory questions and topics. May be used with Spoken English or separately. Questions and topics correspond. Fresh and beautiful selections from best authors. 384 pages. $1.25; to teachers, $1.10, postpaid.

The Smile. Introduction to action through an example. $1.00. To members of The Morning League, $0.75, postpaid.

How to Add Ten Years to Your Life. Nature of training with short, practical program. $1.00. To members of The Morning League, $0.75, postpaid.

Write to Dr. Curry about the Morning League; Summer Terms; Home Studies; School of Expression; new books, or for advice regarding your life work. Address: Book Department, School of Expression, 308 Pierce Bldg., Copley Square, Boston, Mass.